Are you looking for something you can put on in the morning before you go to work and have it ready for supper?

Try:
Apricot Chicken p.139
Guiness® Pot Roast p.111
Kansas Stew p.45
Onion Soup p.37
Green Chile Stew p.43
Swiss Steak p.96
Kate's Cola Chicken p.130
Caribbean Black Beans p.165
Posole p.163

Do you want to pick up a few things on the way home and have dinner ready in an hour?

Try:
Oyster Stew p.36
Baked Eggs p.49
Spaghetti Carbonara p.62
Quiche Nita Rose p.64
Fish & Vegetable Skillet p.74
Beef Strips in Sour Cream p.106
Lamb Curry p.124
Chicken & Ham Almondine p.131

Do you want to have guests for a dinner that is elegant but easy?

Try:
Steak Bobs p.87
Wine Pork Roast p.112
Kathy's Green Chile Chicken p.141
Roast Leg of Lamb p.129
Pork Chops with Apple Schnapps p.118
Chicken Merelyn p.137

How about a menu that is either ready to serve ahead of time or cooks in the oven while you visit?

Try:
Red Bell Soup Mollie p.38
Oven Bar-be-que p.90
Oven Baked Vegetables p.161
July Fourth Salad p.221
Apple Almond Crisp p.251

or:

Borscht p.41
Original Brisket p.94
Baked Beans p.166
Cole Slaw p.218
Lemon Ginger Sherbet p.258

COOKING with a HANDFUL of Ingredients

DELICIOUS MEALS IN THE PALM OF YOUR HAND

By Agnesa & Jack Reeve

First Edition

 Cimarron Press, Santa Fe, New Mexico

Cooking with a Handful of Ingredients

Delicious Meals in the Palm of Your Hand

By Agnesa & Jack Reeve

Published by:

CIMARRON PRESS
Santa Fe, New Mexico
U.S.A.

First Printing 1992

ISBN 0-9631401-6-7

Library of Congress Catalog Card No. 91-77268

Printed in the United States of America

Table of Contents

Serenely full, the epicure would say,
Fate cannot harm me, I have dined today.

Rev. Sydney Smith, 1855

Acknowledgement

We gratefully acknowledge the enthusiastic help we have had from family and friends who contributed their own favorite recipes, tested some of ours, speculated with us on the ingredients in mysterious restaurant dishes, and cheerfully consumed innumerable dinners consisting principally of culinary experiments.

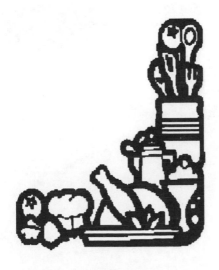

This book is designed to provide eating pleasure. The authors and Cimarron Press, however, shall have neither liability or responsibility to any person or entity with respect to any loss or damage caused, or alleged to be caused, directly or indirectly by the information contained in this book.

ABOUT THE BOOK . . .

COOKING WITH A HANDFUL OF INGREDIENTS is dedicated to the idea that marvelous food does not have to be complicated. These recipes call for a handful - five - ingredients, plus salt, pepper, and butter (margarine, cooking oil). In some cases, there are one or two optional flourishes.

Some dishes are intrinsically simple; others are based on more elaborate recipes, modified to give a similar result.

You will find most types of food represented, but if a recipe has twenty-three ingredients, six of which can be found only in a Baluchistanian native market, it won't be here.

Considerable thought has been given to minimizing calories and cholesterol when that can be done without jeopardizing the character of the dish. It is not always possible - Green Chile Bisque, like any bisque, must be made with cream.

ABOUT THE RECIPES . . .

Creativity is part of the satisfaction in cooking. Variations have been suggested for many dishes -let your imagination supply your own versions.

Wine means the drinking variety, though not necessarily expensive. So-called cooking wine will not do - it has so much added salt it will ruin your dish.

When a recipe calls for butter, it usually can mean butter-flavored margarine or cooking oil. A "greased" or "buttered" baking dish may be sprayed with a vegetable cooking spray in most cases.

You may add your own dash of flavor if you stock a few things besides plain salt and pepper and cooking oil: olive oil, garlic salt or powder, lemon pepper, basil, thyme and tarragon.

In recipes that mention cream, you can substitute milk, even low-fat (but not low-lactose), recognizing the loss of both texture and flavor.

When we give microwave or processor instructions, it is because it is simpler. In the case of microwave, you can substitute the range top. It is more difficult to replace the processor, but a blender, or even grinder and sieve will reward the determined.

Almost all of the recipes will work well if doubled.

Your oven should always be preheated to the specified temperature.

APPETIZERS

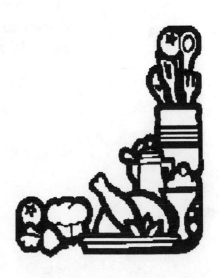

Appetizers, one of the categories of food the most fun to concoct, may be used as they are named, for an appetizing prelude to a dinner, or they may round out the buffet table, or stand in as a meal at a cocktail party or informal gathering.

The choice of hors d'oeuvres is almost infinite in taste, elaborateness, and expense. For example, if you are feeling extravagant, you can buy 3 or 4 pounds of already cooked fresh shrimp, spread it over the ice in a punch bowl and provide toothpicks and a bowl of bottled cocktail sauce. You may want to add the juice of a lemon and a few drops of Tabasco® to the sauce.

If your purse feels light, on the other hand, cut some celery and carrot sticks, and broccoli florets, and serve with mayonaisse spiced with fresh dill, lemon juice and pepper.

Most of the recipes that follow assume you do not have someone to pass among your guests with successive trays of hot tidbits. Therefore, although they can be passed, they are dips or bites to which people may help themselves.

RED & HOT BEAN DIP

2 15-oz cans red kidney beans, drained
1/2 lb Provolone cheese, grated
2 to 4 jalapeños, according to taste
1/4 medium onion, chopped
1 clove garlic, mashed

1/4 lb butter

Put beans, jalapeños, onion and garlic in processor and mix until beans are pureed, but the texture coarse. Heat bean mixture with butter and cheese until cheese is melted. Keep hot in a chafing dish and serve with corn chips. Makes about 1 quart.

This is a spicy change from chili con queso, and can be hot or mild, depending on the amount of jalapeño you use. (If you are not sure, start with 1 and taste. The heat in any pepper is in the seeds and membranes.)

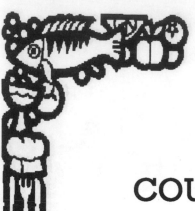

COUNTRY PATÉ

1 lb chicken livers
1 medium onion, chopped
1 tsp fines herbes (thyme, rosemary)
12 large fresh mushrooms, chopped
1/4 cup brandy

1/2 tsp salt, 1/8 tsp pepper
1/4 lb butter

Melt butter in a large skillet, and cook livers and onion over medium heat about 10 minutes, stirring constantly. Add fines herbes and mushrooms; stir and cook 5 minutes longer. Put mixture in processor with brandy, salt and pepper; process until pureed but still a coarse texture. Pack in a 2-cup crock or dish and chill thoroughly. To serve, garnish with parsley and provide toast. Sweet little gherkins are nice with it, too.

If covered tightly, paté may be kept in refrigerator up to a week.

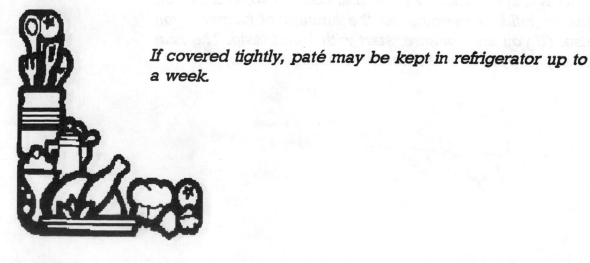

MAJOR GREY'S DIP

1/2 lb liverwurst, room temperature
4 TBS Major Grey's chutney
1 tsp creamy horseradish sauce

Salt to taste

Blend chutney and horseradish sauce with liverwurst.
Add salt to taste. Serve with thin-sliced pumpernickel.

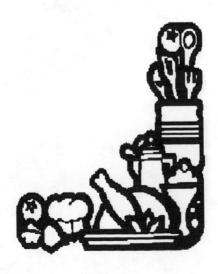

BEEF BITES

2 lbs good quality, aged, steak
2 TBS dry mustard
1 tsp garlic salt
1/4 cup red wine
2 tsp Worcestershire sauce

1/2 cup (1 stick) butter

Broil steak medium rare (NOT well done). Cut into bite-size pieces, about 1/2-inch cubes.
Heat remaining ingredients and pour over steak bites.
Toss to coat bites; keep hot in chafing dish, and provide toothpicks.

This is a wonderful buffet dish that also works with ham bites.

CLAM DIP

1 8-oz carton yogurt
1 7 1/2-oz can minced clams, drained
1 tsp lemon juice
1 tsp Worcestershire sauce

Mix lemon juice and Worcestershire with yogurt. Stir in clams. Chill. Serve with crackers or potato chips. Makes about 3 cups.

You can use cream cheese or sour cream instead of yogurt if calories are no consideration.

With any mild-flavored recipe like this one, use the small inner leaves of endive as dippers. Besides being crisp and flavorful, they look attractive surrounding the bowl.

DARTMOUTH DIP

1 cup mayonaisse
1/2 mild onion, grated
1 cup sharp or mild cheese, grated

Something to dip with: crackers, chips, etc.

(Mix ahead of time if you like, and keep in refrigerator.) Mix all ingredients. If you use a processor, leave the texture coarse. Bake in a small crock (4 or 5 inch diameter) at 350^0 for 15 minutes. Serve hot.

Slices of jicama or apple are good with this.

CRAB DIP

1 8-oz cream cheese, softened
1 can flaked crab meat
1 tsp Worcestershire sauce
Mayonaisse as needed

Stir crab meat into softened cream cheese. Add Worcestershire sauce. Add mayonaisse until mixture is of dip consistency.

Celery sticks and slices or sticks of jicama as well as potato chips make good dippers.

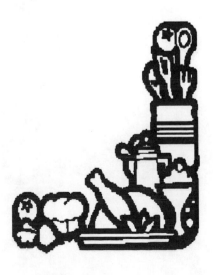

CHEESE OLIVE BALLS

1 jar Old English® sharp cheese spread
1 to 1 1/2 cups sifted flour
Small stuffed olives

1 stick margarine (NOT butter), softened

Cream margarine and cheese. Sift in flour to consistency of ice box cookie dough.
Shape in round patties and fold around stuffed olives.
Bake at 450⁰ for 15 to 20 minutes. Serve hot. Makes 40 to 50 balls.

These may be made, up to baking, the day before, or may be frozen.

BOURSIN CHEESE DIP

1 3-oz pkg cream cheese, softened
2 TBS freshly grated Parmesan cheese
1 TBS dry white wine
1 TBS minced parsley
1/2 tsp fines herbes (thyme, marjoram)

4 TBS butter, softened

In processor, blend all ingredients until smooth. Chill 4 hours or longer; serve with chips, crackers, or melba toast. Makes 1 cup.

For cucumber sandwiches, trim crusts from white bread, spread with this cheese mixture, and top with slices of peeled cucumber. Make plenty!

CALCUTTA SPREAD

2 8-oz pkgs cream cheese, room temperature
1/2 cup Major Grey's chutney
1/2 cup chopped almonds
1 tsp curry powder
1/2 tsp dry mustard

Mix all ingredients - hand mixing is better than the processor. Pack in a 3-cup crock or dish; cover and chill.

This is a delicious spread for crackers or as celery stuffing.

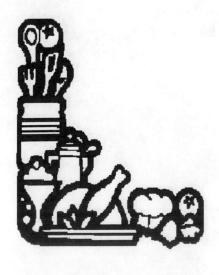

CHEESY POTATO SKINS

2 large russet potatoes
1/4 lb sharp cheddar, shredded

4 TBS butter, melted

Bake potatoes until done and skin is hardened. (Microwave does not work because it leaves the skins soft.) Slice in two lengthwise; remove pulp. With a sharp knife, cut each shell half in four strips (eighths). Paint inside of strips with melted butter; sprinkle with cheese. Broil, 4 inches from heat, for 5 minutes or until cheese is melted and starting to brown. Makes 16 snacks.

PARTY RYE

1 cup Swiss cheese, grated
2 slices bacon, cooked crisp
2 tsp Worcestershire sauce
1/4 cup mayonaisse
I loaf party rye bread

Crumble bacon and mix with cheese, Worcestershire, and mayonaisse. Spread on slices of small party rye. Bake slices at 375⁰ for 10 to 15 minutes until brown, and serve hot. Makes 36.

You can make these ahead and freeze, then reheat.

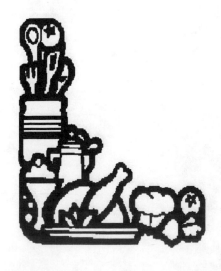

ANTIPASTO ROBUSTO

1 head romaine, or other sharp salad greens
2 red bell peppers
1 lb kielbasa sausage
4 oz fresh mushrooms
6 oz mozzarella cheese, whole

Wash and trim greens. Core and seed red peppers; cut lengthwise in eighths. Clean mushrooms with a damp paper towel and slice. Cut mozzarella into 8 slices.
Score sausage diagonally on both sides and place on baking sheet. Broil 4 inches from heat for 7 to 8 minutes or until kielbasa is brown on both sides.
Arrange romaine leaves around outside of serving plate. Leaving an inch or two of greens showing, top with a layer of pepper slices, wider ends pointing out. Layer mozzarella slices over narrow ends of peppers.

Cut kielbasa into diagonal 1-inch slices and pile in center of plate. Drizzle with vinaigrette. Serves 4 as an entree.

For its own special vinaigrette:
1 small bunch Italian parsley, chopped; 1 clove garlic, mashed; 1 1/2 TBS balsamic vinegar; 1/2 TBS Dijon mustard; 1/8 cup olive oil. Mix thoroughly.

SALMON ROLL

1 14-oz can salmon
1 8-oz pkg cream cheese, softened
1 TBS horseradish sauce
2 TBS lemon juice
Juice from a large onion

Salt & pepper
OPTIONAL: pecan pieces

Drain salmon. Remove skin and large bones.
Extract juice from onion by cutting it in half and using a fruit reamer (a saucer with a ribbed cone in its center.)
Combine salmon, cream cheese, horseradish sauce, lemon juice and onion juice; taste and add salt and pepper as needed, or more horseradish sauce. Mix thoroughly. Shape into a roll about 2" diameter. Place flat on a plate and cover. Chill at least 4 hours. Roll in pecan pieces if desired. Return to refrigerator and chill overnight. It does not get very firm. Serve with melba toast. Serves 8 or more as an appetizer.

CEVICHE

2 cups shrimp, cleaned & deveined
1/2 cup finely chopped onion
1/2 cup finely chopped tomatoes
2 TBS fresh lime juice
1 TBS Worcestershire sauce

Combine all ingredients lightly but thoroughly. Cover
and chill for at least 15 minutes - an hour is better.
Serve cold in tall glasses, like tapered beer glasses.
Serves 4.

*Other seafood may be used with or instead of shrimp -
crab, fish bites, lobster, etc. A wonderful addition is
chopped avocado, and a teaspoon of cilantro.*

BARBARA'S 4-STAR GUACAMOLE

2 large avocados, mashed
1 small onion, grated
1 4 oz can chopped mild green chile
1 FRESHLY hard-cooked egg
2 TBS mayonaisse

1/3 stick of butter, softened
Salt

Mix avocado with onion and green chile.
Grate warm egg over butter and work in the mayonaisse with a whisk. Gradually add avocado mixture. Taste and add salt as necessary.
Makes about 1 1/2 cups, but it is so good it is never enough!

To keep your guacamole from turning brown, add 1/2 can of commercial frozen guacamole to your mix. You can use 2 cans of frozen guacamole in place of the fresh avocados.

For a simple guacamole that is also delicious, simply mash the avocados, add the juice of a lemon, salt and pepper, and a few drops of Tabasco®.

FRESH GREEN SALSA

1/2 cup finely chopped mild green chile
1/2 cup finely chopped tomatoes
1 medium onion chopped (or green onions)
1 clove garlic, mashed

1/2 tsp salt

Combine all ingredients and chill for 1 hour or more. Makes about 1 cup.

Among the ingredients often added to the basic salsa are 1 tablespoon of chopped fresh cilantro, or 1 tablespoon of wine vinegar, or 1/2 or more chopped jalapeño for a hotter sauce.

In the Southwest, the standard but always welcome "before" is Salsa and Chips - fresh salsa served with corn tortilla chips for dipping.

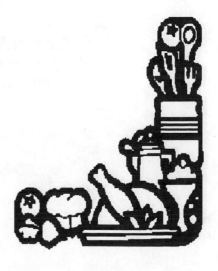

HORSERADISH MOLD

1 envelope unflavored gelatin
1/2 cup Miracle Whip® (NOT mayonnaise)
1/3 cup cream-style horseradish sauce
1 cup whipping cream

1/4 tsp salt

OPTIONAL: stuffed olives & paprika for garnish

Soften gelatin in 3/4 cup cold water. Heat until gelatin dissolves. Mix salad dressing, horseradish and salt until smooth. Combine with gelatin. Whip cream until stiff; fold into horseradish mixture. Pour mixture into a 1-quart mold (either ring or solid mold). Refrigerate overnight.

To serve, unmold on lettuce and garnish with slices of stuffed olives and paprika, if desired.

For a buffet, slice the mold in 1/4-inch thick slices, and on a platter alternate with slightly overlapping slices of meat - beef, ham, corned beef.

SOUPS & STEWS

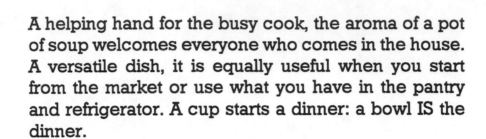

A helping hand for the busy cook, the aroma of a pot of soup welcomes everyone who comes in the house. A versatile dish, it is equally useful when you start from the market or use what you have in the pantry and refrigerator. A cup starts a dinner: a bowl IS the dinner.

From a delicate broth to hearty stew, hot or cold, a soup depends on a blend of flavors. If you start with a canned or packaged soup mix you can usually improve it with the addition of the spices you prefer, such as garlic or onion powder for meat soups, or basil and thyme for vegetable. A cup of chopped celery and a handful of minced parsley or chives often enliven the bowl.

If you substitute dry boullion for chicken or beef broth, be sure to use the salt-free variety. The standard boullion cube contains too much salt for health or taste. If you can, keep a couple of cans of ready-to-use broth on your shelf.

SEAFOOD CHOWDER

1/2 lb seafood (shrimp, fake crab, fish)
2 cups milk
2 TBS flour
1 onion, finely chopped
Grated zest of 1 lemon

3 TBS butter
Salt & pepper

Make a thin cream sauce: over medium heat, melt butter in skillet; whisk in flour till bubbly; add milk slowly, whisking constantly. Stir in onion and seafood. Salt and pepper to taste. Lower heat, cover and simmer 15 minutes.
To serve, sprinkle with lemon zest. Serves 2.

Zest is the thin yellow rind (or orange in the case of oranges) without any white pulp. The zest has the flavor and the pulp is bitter. To peel, use a vegetable parer with a light touch.

GREEN SOUP

1 cup chopped broccoli florets, or chopped
    spinach
2 cups milk
2 TBS flour

3 TBS butter
Salt & pepper

Make a thin cream sauce: over medium heat, melt
butter in skillet; whisk in flour till bubbly; add milk
slowly, whisking constantly. Stir in broccoli or
spinach. Salt and pepper to taste. Lower heat, cover
and simmer 30 minutes. Serves 2.

*The same recipe will work with 1 cup of other
vegetables, too: green peas, or chopped tomatoes or
celery, for example.*

SHRIMP & CORN CHOWDER

1/2 lb shrimp, shelled & deveined
1 10-oz pkg frozen corn, thawed
1 can cream of mushroom soup, undiluted
1 red bell pepper, chopped
1 tsp Worcestershire sauce

Salt & pepper
1/2 soup can of water

Combine corn, soup, water, bell pepper and Worcestershire in saucepan, bring to boil and simmer 5 to 10 minutes. Add shrimp to boiling mixture and simmer 5 minutes more. Salt and pepper to taste. Serves 4.

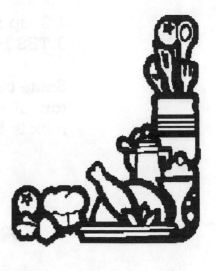

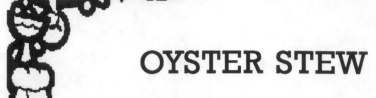

OYSTER STEW

MICROWAVE

1 8-oz can oysters, or 1/2 pint oysters
1/2 to 3/4 cup milk
Dash of paprika
2 TBS butter

Drain oysters and reserve liquid.
Melt butter on HIGH, 30 to 45 seconds. Add drained oysters. Cover and microwave on HIGH 2 to 4 minutes. The edges will curl.
Put oyster liquid in a 2-cup measure and add milk to make 1 1/2 cups. Combine with oysters; microwave on MEDIUM-HIGH 4 to 6 minutes. Sprinkle with paprika. Serves 2.

DOUBLE BOILER

1 8-oz can oysters, or 1/2 pint oysters, undrained
1 1/2 cups milk
1/2 cup cream
1/8 tsp paprika
1 tsp grated onion

1/2 tsp salt
3 TBS butter

Sauté onion in butter. Add to remaining ingredients in top of double boiler over boiling water. Heat until milk is hot and oysters float. Serves 2-4.

ONION SOUP

3 large onions, chopped
2 cloves garlic, mashed
3 cups beef broth
1 cup cider
3 oz. Swiss cheese, grated

Salt & pepper

Combine onions, garlic, broth, and cider with 1 quart water in a heavy pot. Salt and pepper to taste. Cover and simmer 2 to 3 hours. Serve with cheese sprinkled on top. Serves 6-8.

For two people; use big bowls, have a green salad, a loaf of French bread, and a dry red wine.

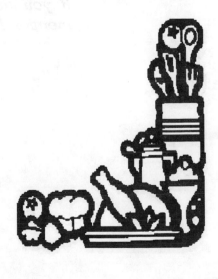

RED BELL SOUP MOLLIE

2 red bell peppers, seeded & chopped
1 cup chopped scallions, white part
1 can ready-to-eat chicken broth
2 cups buttermilk
Chopped parsley for garnish

2 TBS butter

Sauté peppers and scallions in butter. Add chicken broth. Cook down about 30 minutes. Process and puree. Cool. Add buttermilk. Serve cold, garnished with parsley if desired. Or you can sprinkle it with paprika.
Serves 4.

If you think someone might not like buttermilk, don't mention it. They'll never know.

GAZPACHO

1 quart Snappy Tom® spicy tomato juice
2 cucumbers, peeled
1/4 cup wine vinegar
1 TBS sugar
1/4 cup chopped green onions

Combine half of Snappy Tom® with other ingredients in processor. Blend well. Transfer to large bowl and stir in remaining juice. Taste for flavor. If you used juice other than Snappy Tom® you may want to add salt, pepper and Tabasco®. Chill and serve very cold. Serves 6.

Snappy Tom® can be replaced with Spicy Hot V-8® or Mr.& Mrs.T's® Bloody Mary mix.

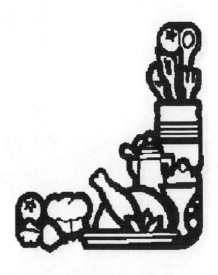

VICHYSSOISE

2 cups peeled, sliced potatoes
2 cups sliced onions
4 1/2 cups chicken broth
1/2 cup cream
2 TBS minced chives

Salt & pepper

Simmer the potatoes and onions in broth until thoroughly done.
Puree with liquid in processor. Stir in cream, and season to taste. Chill several hours or overnight.
Serve in chilled soup cups; sprinkle with chives.
Serves 4 to 6.

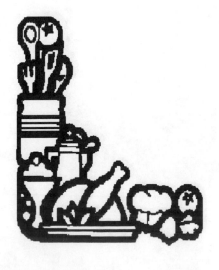

BORSCHT

1 15-oz can beets, undrained
1 lemon, juiced
2 cups chicken broth
1 cup plain yogurt or sour cream
1 purple onion, grated

Salt & pepper

In processor, combine beets with liquid, onion, lemon juice, and broth. Puree. Salt and pepper to taste. Chill for several hours in covered dish. Serve very cold; put about 1/4 cup of yogurt or sour cream in center of each bowl of borscht. Serves 4 to 6.

A colorful and delicious way to begin a summer meal.

GREEN CHILE BISQUE

1/4 cup chopped mild green chile
2 TBS finely minced onion
2 TBS flour
3/4 cup light cream (not milk)
1 cup chicken broth

3 TBS butter
Salt & pepper

Melt the butter in a heavy saucepan and sauté the onion briefly. Whisk flour into butter mixture. Add chile (with liquid). Stir in cream and chicken broth. Lower heat and simmer 10 minutes. stirring frequently. Salt and pepper to taste. Serves 2.

GREEN CHILE STEW

2 lbs hamburger
1 lb mild green chile, chopped
3 large onions, chopped
2 cups instant mashed potatoes
2 cups beef broth

In large pot or Dutch oven, brown hamburger and drain. Add chile, onions and broth. Add sufficient water to cover. Cover and simmer 1 hour or more. Before serving add instant potatoes to thicken stew. Serves 8.

SPRINGER GREEN CHILE

3 large onions, chopped
3 large potatoes, chopped
2 lbs hamburger
1 lb mild green chile, chopped
Salt

Boil onions and potatoes together in water to cover until both disintegrate, making a thick soup. Brown hamburger; add chile and potato mixture. Salt to taste. Simmer together 15 to 20 minutes. Serves 8.

There are a hundred green chile stew recipes, but these keep to the basics: meat, onions, and chile. Incidentally, in case they are available in your area, the frozen chile has a better flavor than canned. These peppers are sometimes spelled chili, with an i.

IRISH LAMB STEW

2 lbs lamb breast or shoulder, diced
2 onions, coarsely chopped
8 small potatoes, whole, unpeeled
1/2 head cabbage, coarsely chopped
1 cup cooked green peas

Salt & pepper to taste

Simmer lamb in water to cover; skim off any scum. Add onions. When meat is tender, add potatoes and continue simmering. When the potatoes are almost tender, add cabbage and cook 15 minutes longer. Salt and pepper to taste. Before serving, sprinkle with peas. Serves 4.

KANSAS BEEF STEW

1 lb lean beef (a cheap cut is OK)
1 lb potatoes
1 large onion
4 stalks celery
4 small carrots

Salt & pepper

Cut up beef and vegetables into 1-inch pieces. Place in large, heavy pot; add water to cover. Salt and pepper to taste. Bring to boil; lower heat, cover pot closely and simmer 2 to 4 hours. Serves 4 to 6.

With hot cornbread and a green salad, this makes a wonderful cold weather supper.

SCOTTISH PUB BROTH

1 lb lamb (beef, pork) finely cut up
1/3 cup barley
2 onions, finely chopped
2 carrots or 3 stalks celery, chopped
2 tsp Worcestershire sauce

Butter
Salt & pepper

In a large heavy pot, brown lamb in butter. Add salt and pepper to taste. Add 2 quarts water, bring to boil and stir in barley. Lower heat, cover, and simmer 2 hours, stirring occasionally to keep barley from sticking. Add vegetables and continue simmering until they are tender but not overcooked. Add water if necessary. Add Worcestershire sauce (and more salt and pepper if needed.) Serves 6.

Every Scottish pub has a "Today's Broth" - it is never the same as the last broth, but always delicious. They, and you, may use a beef, pork, or chicken base in place of lamb. The ingredient that identifies it as Scottish broth is the barley.

EGGS,
PASTA,
CHEESE

Sometimes called "luncheon dishes," these lighter entrees are equally welcome for supper.

More interesting than poached-eggs-on-toast, a choice from this section makes a very pleasant main dish and a satisfying meal accompanied, in most cases, by no more than a green salad or sliced tomatoes and a special bread - muffins, cornbread, French bread, etc.

Many of these dishes - omelet, quiche, pasta, soufflé - lend themselves to encompassing the leftovers you have in the refrigerator. Chop vegetables or meats in small pieces, perhaps add a chopped onion, tomato or seasonings and concoct an original.

BAKED EGGS

4 large ripe tomatoes
1/4 cup chopped fresh parsley
4 eggs
Basil
Parmesan or cheddar cheese, grated

1 tsp butter, diced
Salt & pepper

Hollow out tomatoes, reserving pulp for some other use. Place shells in buttered baking dish and sprinkle hollows with salt, pepper and parsley. (To this point you can prepare ahead, in case you have guests coming for brunch.)
Bake shells uncovered at 400⁰ for 5 minutes, then break an egg into each tomato shell and top with butter and basil. Bake (still uncovered) 15 minutes. Sprinkle with cheese and return to oven for 5 minutes. Serves 4.

As long as your oven is going to be hot for half an hour, you might put 4 slices of ham in a shallow baking dish to heat while you cook the eggs. Add 1/4 cup of orange juice (or water) to keep the ham from drying out.

SCRAMBLED EGGS

Following amounts PER PERSON:

2 eggs
1 TBS cream

1/2 TBS butter

Stir eggs and cream together. Melt butter in small skillet over medium heat. Pour in eggs and sauté, stirring gently until desired doneness.
You will have better luck if you do not try to scramble more than 6 eggs at one time. If you must cook more, use a lower heat and a large stirring spoon.

For innumerable variations on the above, add chopped cooked bacon, grated cheese, or any of the ingredients suggested for an omelet.

UNIVERSAL OMELET

3 eggs
1 TBS flour
1 TBS milk
1 TBS shredded cheese

2 TBS butter, softened

Mix first 4 ingredients with 1 tablespoon butter. Heat remaining butter in small skillet over medium heat. Pour in egg mixture. When edges bubble, lift edge at several places with spatula and tilt skillet to let liquid egg run under to cook. Continue until omelet is firm but not dry, 2 or 3 minutes.
Slide omelet onto warm plate, folding over to reveal golden brown underside. Serves 1 or 2, depending on appetites.

FOR VARIETY; many ingredients can be placed in the center of the omelet as it cooks, then folded into middle when the omelet is turned from pan: bacon pieces, avocado, ham, salsa or picante sauce, etc. Also, you can include something like diced avocado in the omelet, then cover with salsa to serve.

A sweet omelet is a good supper dish. Use diced cream cheese, chunky pineapple or other fruit inside, and top with marmalade or fruit preserves.

FRENCH TOAST

Amounts PER PERSON:

1 egg
2 slices bread

1 to 2 TBS butter

Beat eggs until frothy. Dip bread slices in egg, hold up on fork to let drain. Fry on both sides in butter until golden brown.

Three-quarter inch thick slices of homemade-type bread make the best toast, but any bread, white or wheat, will do.

Syrup is, of course, the expected sauce for French toast, but you may like it even better with fruit preserves or fresh fruit puree. Even fancier, spread toast with mashed fresh strawberries, for example, and top with whipped topping and 3 fresh strawberries for garnish.

HUEVOS RANCHEROS WITH SALSA I

1/2 cup chopped onion
1 clove garlic, minced
3 large tomatoes, chopped finely
1 4-oz can chopped mild green chile,
    undrained
6 eggs

Butter
TO SERVE:
6 corn tortillas, heated
1/2 cup shredded Monterey Jack or cheddar
    cheese

In a small saucepan, cook onion and garlic in 1 TBS butter until onion is tender, 2 or 3 minutes. Add tomatoes and chile with liquid and heat thoroughly.

Poach eggs or fry lightly in butter.
Place hot tortilla on a plate, put fried egg on it, and top with sauce. Sprinkle with cheese.

If you like your sauce hotter, add Tabasco® to taste.

Another method: put the tortillas in a baking dish, cover with tomato mixture. Form 6 hollows in tomato layer and break an egg into each. Cover. Bake at 350º for 25 minutes. Sprinkle with cheese and return to oven just long enough for cheese to melt, 1 to 2 minutes.

HUEVOS RANCHEROS SALSA II

8 slices thick-cut bacon, chopped
1 large onion, thinly sliced
1 clove garlic, mashed
1 4-oz can chopped mild green chile
2 cups chopped tomatoes, fresh or canned

Salt and pepper

In a heavy skillet, fry bacon over medium-low heat; drain, retaining 1 teaspoon fat. Add onion and garlic and cook 2 to 3 minutes. Add chile, tomatoes, salt and pepper. Simmer 20 minutes.

For a hotter sauce, use medium green chile, or add one or two chopped jalapeño peppers, or a few drops of Tabasco®.

SCOTCH EGGS

6 hard-boiled eggs, peeled & hot
2 eggs, well beaten
1 lb bulk sausage
1 cup breadcrumbs or cornmeal

Cooking oil

Combine 1/2 the beaten eggs with sausage and mix well. Divide into 6 portions. Cover each egg with 1/6 of sausage mixture, patting firmly around entire egg. Dip meat-encased eggs in remaining egg mixture, and roll each in crumbs. In a heavy skillet, heat 1/2 inch oil and fry eggs, turning them often to brown on all sides. Sausage should be dark brown. Drain well on paper towels; chill overnight before serving. Makes 6 servings.

When you are taking a dish to a picnic, surprise them with these - or add them to a brunch buffet.

EGG AND SALMON SCRAMBLE

5 eggs
1/2 cup shredded smoked salmon
1/4 cup minced onion
1/4 cup red bell pepper, finely chopped
1 Roma (small) tomato, chopped

2 TBS butter

Sauté onion and pepper until soft. Beat eggs. Mix eggs with other ingredients. In non-stick pan, melt butter and cook mixture, stirring gently over medium heat until done.
Serves 2.

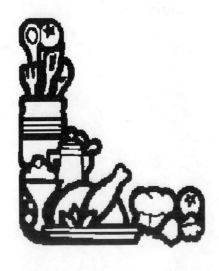

GARLIC CHEESE GRITS

1 cup uncooked quick grits
6 oz garlic cheese, cut up
1/2 cup milk
2 eggs, well beaten

1/2 cup (1 stick) butter, cut up

Cook grits according to directions on package.
Stir cheese and butter into hot grits until melted.
Combine milk and beaten eggs; stir into grits. In a
buttered 8"x11" baking dish, bake uncovered at 350°
for 45 minutes to 1 hour, or until mixture is set and
golden. Serves 4 to 6.

Even Yankees like these grits!
This recipe doubled is great for a crowd - increase
cooking time by 30 minutes.

FETTUCINE ALFREDO

8 oz uncooked fettucine
1/2 cup grated Parmesan cheese
1/3 cup cream

1/4 cup butter, softened
Salt & pepper

Cook noodles according to package directions. Over low heat, put them in a pre-heated casserole. Add cheese, cream and butter gradually, tossing gently to combine as you add. Season to taste.
Serves 2.

For FETTUCINE EDUARDO, a New Mexico variation, mound 1/4 cup of mild or medium hot chopped green chilis in the center of each serving.

FETTUCINE WITH POPPY SEEDS

3/4 tsp garlic salt
3/4 tsp dried parsley flakes
1 tsp poppy seeds
1/2 cup plain nonfat yogurt
1/2 cup grated Parmesan cheese

1/3 cup butter, melted
Pepper

(8 oz. uncooked fettucine)

Cook fettucine according to package directions. Meanwhile, combine melted butter with garlic salt, parsley, poppy seeds and pepper to taste. Stir in yogurt. Combine with fettucine. Add cheese and toss. Serves 4.

An interesting change from potatoes to go with beef or pork chops, for example.

ROMANO CREAM SAUCE FOR PASTA

4 slices thick-cut bacon, chopped
4 green onions, chopped
1/2 cup cream
1/2 cup freshly grated Romano or Parmesan
   cheese
1/3 cup chopped fresh basil

Salt & pepper
(8 oz uncooked fettuccini)

Cook pasta according to package directions. Meanwhile, fry bacon in heavy skillet over medium heat until almost crisp. Add green onions and stir 2 to 3 minutes. Remove bacon and onion and drain skillet, retaining 1 teaspoon fat. Return bacon and onions to pan; add cream. Stir and simmer until it starts to thicken, about 1 minute. Mix in cheese and basil and toss with hot pasta.
Serves 4.

LINGUINI WITH GREEN SAUCE

4 oz. Parmesan cheese, freshly grated
10-oz pkg frozen chopped spinach
8 oz ricotta cheese
1 TBS fresh lemon juice
2 green onions, chopped

(8 oz uncooked linguini)

Cook spinach according to package directions and drain. In processor, blend spinach and ricotta until smooth. In top of double boiler, stir cheese and lemon juice into spinach mixture.
Cook linguini in boiling salted water (6 cups water with 2 teaspoons salt) until tender but firm, about 8 to 10 minutes. Drain. Toss with green sauce and top with chopped onions. Serves 4 to 6.

Sliced tomatoes paired with the green sauce decorate your plate and palate.

SPAGHETTI CARBONARA

1/2 lb bacon, chopped (or 1/2 lb bulk
   sausage)
1 onion, chopped
2 eggs, well beaten
1/2 cup grated Romano (or Parmesan) cheese
8 oz spaghetti

Cook bacon or sausage with onions until meat is done. Drain off grease; cover, keep hot over lowest heat. Cook spaghetti in boiling salted water (2 teaspoons salt to 6 cups water) until tender but firm, about 8 to 10 minutes. Drain. Quickly mix beaten eggs into hot spaghetti. Stir in cheese. Add meat mixture and toss. Serve immediately.
Serves 4.

Eggs must be cooked in some way before eating to avoid danger of salmonella, which means they must reach 160 degrees. This is the reason for being sure the spaghetti is piping hot when you add the eggs and cheese.

Spaghetti with a meat sauce is the ideal dinner for the working cook - working outside the kitchen, that is. On the way home from the office, just pick up the ingredients plus a head of romaine lettuce, a loaf of French bread and a bottle of cabernet savignon.

WELSH RAREBIT

1/2 tsp Dijon mustard
2 tsp Worcestershire sauce
1 lb sharp PROCESSED cheese, grated
1 cup beer
2 eggs. slightly beaten

4 TBS butter
Salt & pepper

Melt butter, seasonings and cheese in top of double boiler over hot water. Stir until cheese is melted and add 1/2 cup beer, a tablespoon at a time. Mix eggs with a little more beer and add to the cheese, stirring until smooth. Add beer to proper consistency. (You may not need all the beer.) Serve on thick French bread toast, or on slices of broiled tomatoes, or on toast topped with tomatoes. Serves 6.

All you want with a rarebit is a salad of greens, lightly dressed with oil, vinegar, salt and pepper.

QUICHE NITA ROSE

3 eggs
1/4 to 1/2 cup cream
Dash of nutmeg
1 1/2 to 2 cups optional ingredients
Unbaked pie shell

1 TBS butter
Salt & pepper

OPTIONAL: one or more of following:
Chopped cooked ham, grated cheese, chopped spinach, green chile, onions or mixed vegetables

Bake pie shell at 450⁰ for 7 to 10 minutes.
Break the eggs into a 2 cup measure. Add cream to 1 1/4 cup volume. Whisk in salt, pepper and nutmeg. Put optional ingredients of your choice in the bottom of pie shell. Pour eggs over and dot with butter.
Bake at 375⁰ for 30 minutes. Serves 4 to 6.

BAKED SPINACH & CHEESE

1 egg, beaten
1/2 cup biscuit mix
1/2 cup milk
1/2 lb Monterey Jack cheese, grated
4 cups chopped spinach (fresh or frozen,
    thawed)

4 TBS butter

Melt butter in 8" x 8" baking dish. Combine egg, biscuit mix and milk. Reserving 1/4 cup cheese, add remaining cheese and spinach, mixing well. Spoon into baking dish and sprinkle reserved cheese over top. Bake at 350⁰ for 35 minutes.
Serves 4 - 6.

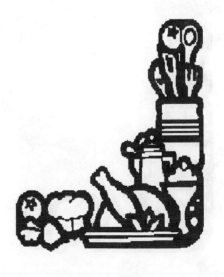

TOMATO TART

Baked 8" or 9" pie shell
1 lb Gruyere cheese, thinly sliced
3 large tomatoes, cut in 1/2" slices
1 tsp dried basil
2 TBS grated Parmesan cheese

Salt & pepper
2 TBS butter, melted

Sprinkle tomato slices with salt and allow them to drain on a rack for about 1/2 hour. In the pastry shell, arrange slightly overlapping Gruyere slices; layer tomato slices on top of cheese. Sprinkle with pepper, basil and Parmesan. Drizzle melted butter over all. Bake at 375⁰ for 25 minutes. Serves 6.

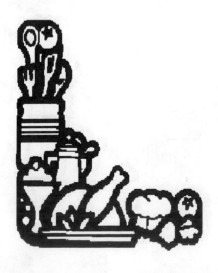

SEAFOOD

Seafood comes in so many guises no general statement applies to every dish.

Tender fillets like sole or tilapia may be broiled or sautéed; slightly less tender such as catfish should be more aggressively fried.

Many different finny and shellfish are most popular when combined with other ingredients in a salad or casserole - crab salad and tuna casserole are among the traditions of American cooking.

Certainly one of the advantages of seafood is that it is usually quite quickly cooked.

CRAB CASSEROLE

2 cups canned or frozen crabmeat
4 slices white bread
1 cup milk
8 hard-cooked eggs, chopped
2 cups mayonaisse

Salt & pepper

OPTIONAL: 2 tsp grated onion
1/4 cup Ritz® cracker crumbs

Soak bread in milk until it breaks apart naturally. Combine bread and milk with crab, eggs, mayonaisse, onion if desired, and salt and pepper to taste. Place in buttered casserole. You may top with crumbs.
Bake uncovered at 350⁰ for 1 hour. Serves 8.

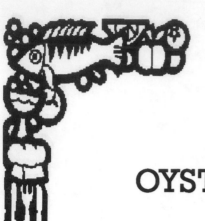

OYSTER CASSEROLE

1/2 pint fresh oysters
1 cup wild & white rice
1 cup green onions, finely chopped
2 cups mushrooms, thinly sliced
1 cup dry white wine

2 TBS butter
Salt & pepper

OPTIONAL: 1/2 cup crushed Ritz® crackers

In a medium sized skillet, sauté onions and mushrooms in butter. Add 1/4 teaspoon salt and 1/8 teaspoon pepper. Cook 5 minutes. Add wine; simmer slowly for another 10 minutes.
Cook rice according to package, and drain. Combine rice with onion-mushroom mixture. Stir in drained oysters. Place in buttered 2-quart casserole.
Sprinkle with salt and pepper to taste. Bake at 350° for 30 minutes. After 20 minutes sprinkle top with cracker crumbs if desired. Serves 6.

Very tasty, but you'll wonder where the oysters went! A salad of fresh fruit, cut up and dressed with lemon juice and honey complements the flavors.

SEAFOOD CASSEROLE

1 cup cooked shrimp (1 can)
1 cup canned crab meat
1 cup celery, chopped
1 cup mayonnaise
Grated onion to taste

Salt and pepper

OPTIONAL: 1/2 cup bread crumbs

Combine first five ingredients. Salt and pepper to taste. Put in baking dish and top with crumbs, if desired. Bake at 350⁰ for 1 hour.
Serves 4.

The tastiest bread crumbs are made by crushing (or processing) Pepperidge Farm® seasoned croutons. Put any extra crumbs in a tightly closed plastic bag and freeze them for the next time.

BROILED FISH FILLETS

Fish fillets, 1 or 2 per person
        Following amounts for 2 servings:
1 TBS chopped green onions
1 TBS fresh lemon juice
1/3 cup sliced almonds
1/2 tsp fresh basil, crushed

Butter

Sauté onions in 2 tablespoons butter; stir in almonds, lemon juice and basil. Brush fillets with butter mixture. Place in oven 4 inches below broiler. Broil, about 3 minutes per side for sole or tilapia, about 5 mimutes per side for halibut. Brush second side with butter mixture when you turn fillets. Spoon nuts from remaining butter mixture onto fillets during last 2 minutes of cooking.

For an elegant entree, steam fresh asparagus until just tender, and arrange each serving of fish on 5 asparagus stalks.

BAKED FISH FILLETS WITH VARIOUS TOPPINGS

1 lb fish fillets

Place fillets in greased pan and cover with one of the following:

1. 1/2 cup mayonaisse
   1/2 cup sour cream
   2 teaspoons chopped green onion including
      tops

2. 1 cup sour cream
   2 TBS anchovy paste

3. 3/4 cup mayonaisse
   1/2 cup grated Parmesan

With any of these choices, cover with Ritz® cracker crumbs or dry bread crumbs and bake uncovered at 350⁰ for 10 minutes. Serves 4.

FISH & VEGETABLE SKILLET

1 lb fish fillets
4 small new potatoes, unpeeled, halved
2 medium onions, sliced
1 can cream of mushroom soup, undiluted
1 16-oz pkg frozen mixed vegetables

Salt & pepper

OPTIONAL: 1/2 cup white wine

In a large skillet, combine all ingredients except fish. Cover and cook over medium-low heat for 20 minutes. Cut fillets in 1" squares; add to vegetables. Cook 5 minutes or until fish flakes easily. Add wine, if desired, and remove from heat. Serves 2.

A tasty one-dish meal you can put together in half an hour. Especially good with hot cornbread.

BAKED FISH
WITH TOMATOES

6 fillets, sole or tilapia
3 medium tomatoes, finely chopped
1/2 cup chopped green onions
1/2 tsp coriander
1 tsp Hungarian paprika

3 TBS butter, melted

Cover bottom of heavy flat pan with 1 tablespoon of butter. Spread half of tomatoes over pan. Sprinkle onions over tomatoes. Arrange fillets in one layer on top of onions. Cover with remaining tomatoes and sprinkle with coriander. Mix paprika with remaining butter and spoon on each fillet. Cover with foil and bake at 350⁰ for 30 minutes. Serves 3 to 4.

FISH FILLET SAUTÉ

1 lb fish fillets, sole or tilapia
1/2 cup flour
1 egg, well beaten
1 cup bread crumbs, or finely crushed
  crackers

4 TBS butter
Salt & pepper

Mix flour with salt and pepper to taste. Dredge fillets with flour mixture. Dip each fillet in egg, allow surplus to drain off, then coat with crumbs. In hot butter over medium heat, sauté fillets without crowding, about 4 minutes for first side, 3 minutes for second side. Serves 2.

Crumbs made from Ritz® crackers or other seasoned cocktail crackers add flavor. If you have a processor, just throw a few crackers in and whirl them into crumbs. Otherwise, put them in a plastic bag and roll with a rolling pin or bottle.

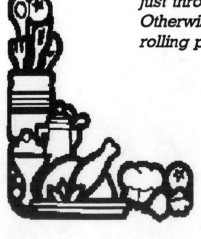

FRIED CATFISH

1 or 2 fish fillets per person
Tabasco® sauce
Yellow cornmeal

Cooking oil

Marinate fillets in undiluted Tabasco® sauce for about an hour. Without drying or over-draining, dredge fillets in cornmeal. Fry in hot oil until flaking, about 4 minutes per side.

This is the best way to cook fish that may have a mossy flavor.

A catfish dinner always means French fries and cole slaw - all you can eat!

FISH WITH GREEN SAUCE

2 lbs sole or tilapia fillets
1 red bell pepper, chopped
3 TBS fresh lemon juice
2 cups fresh or frozen (thawed) chopped
    spinach
2 teaspoons chopped green onion

Salt & pepper

Poach fillets in salted water until fish flakes easily with a fork. Meanwhile, combine remaining ingredients. Microwave on HIGH for 3 minutes, or heat over medium heat, stirring constantly until spinach is cooked.
Serve over fish. Serves 4.

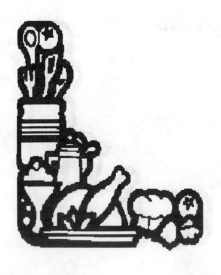

POACHED SALMON

2 fresh salmon steaks
3 TBS vinegar
2 tsp chopped green onions
1 tsp minced fresh dill
2 tsp fresh lemon juice

Salt & pepper
1/2 tsp oil (preferably olive oil)

In a skillet, add 1 1/2 teaspoons salt and 3 tablespoons vinegar to enough water to cover steaks. Bring to boil, add salmon, lower heat and simmer steaks for 10 minutes.
In a small bowl, combine onions, dill, lemon juice, salt and pepper, and oil.
Skin salmon after cooking. To serve, spoon sauce over each steak. Serves 2.

SALMON MOUSSE

1 1-lb can red salmon
1 TBS plain gelatin
2 TBS fresh lemon juice
1/2 cup chili sauce
1/2 cup mayonaisse

Drain salmon. Remove skin and bones, flake finely.
Dissolve gelatin in 1/4 cup cold water. Heat chili
sauce and lemon juice. Stir in gelatin. Remove from
heat, allow to cool; add mayonaisse and salmon.
Mix gently but thoroughly and pack into well-oiled
1-quart mold. Chill overnight. Serves 4.

*Serve the mousse with CUCUMBER SAUCE - 1 medium
cucumber blended in the processor with 1 cup sour
cream and 1/2 teaspoon lemon-pepper - or with
AVOCADO SAUCE - use an avocado instead of
cucumber.*

SALMON PATTIES

1 15-oz can salmon
1 egg
1/3 cup minced onion
1/2 cup flour
1 1/2 tsp baking powder

Salt & pepper
1 1/2 cups oil

Drain salmon, reserving 2 tablespoons juice. Remove skin and bones. Combine salmon, egg and onion. Stir in flour. Add baking powder to salmon juice and stir into salmon mixture. Season to taste. Form into kitchen-spoon-size patties (about 2 tablespoons) and fry in hot oil until golden brown on both sides, about 3 minutes per side.
Serves 4.

TUNA CASSEROLE

2 cups canned tuna
4 hard-cooked eggs, peeled & chopped
1 5-oz pkg potato chips, lightly crushed
1 can cream of mushroom soup
Milk

Add enough milk to soup to make 2 cups. Combine soup mixture with tuna, chopped egg, and 1/2 potato chips. Mix lightly but thoroughly and put in buttered 1-quart casserole. Sprinkle with remaining potato chips. Bake at 325⁰ for 30 minutes.
Serves 4.

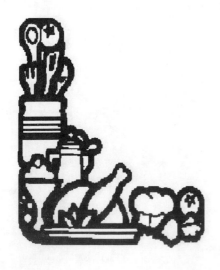

TUNA SALAD

1 6-oz can tuna
1/2 medium onion, grated
1/4 cup chopped dill pickles
3 hard-cooked eggs, chopped
1/2 cup mayonaisse

Salt & pepper

Drain tuna. Combine with next 4 ingredients. Add salt and pepper to taste. Cover and chill.
Serve on lettuce, in tomato shells, or as sandwich filling. Makes 6 to 8 sandwiches or stuffing for 6 tomatoes.

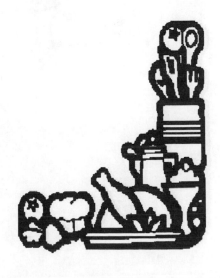

SALMON MOUSSE II

1 1-lb can salmon, drained, flaked
2 envelopes plain gelatin
1 cup mayonaisse
1 cup sour cream
1 cup finely chopped cucumber

Dissolve gelatin in 1 1/2 cups cold water. Heat gently and stir until gelatin dissolves. Combine mayonaisse and sour cream. Stir in gelatin. Chill until slightly thickened. Fold in salmon and cucumber. Pour into lightly oiled 5-cup mold. Chill until firm. To serve, unmold, garnish. Serves 6-8.

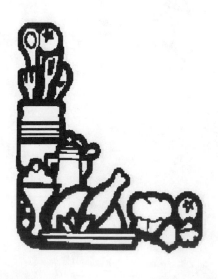

MEATS

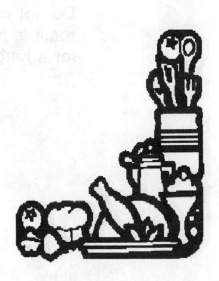

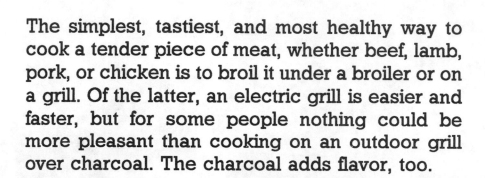

The simplest, tastiest, and most healthy way to cook a tender piece of meat, whether beef, lamb, pork, or chicken is to broil it under a broiler or on a grill. Of the latter, an electric grill is easier and faster, but for some people nothing could be more pleasant than cooking on an outdoor grill over charcoal. The charcoal adds flavor, too.

A dusting of garlic powder and lemon pepper on both sides of the meat before grilling is recommended. Salt before cooking dehydrates the meat somewhat, so sprinkle it on afterward.

Broiling requires a tender, not too large cut of meat, so it is not always appropriate. The suggestions following are for other cuts and other taste experiences.

The basic method for delicious results in cooking large portions of meat - beef, pork, lamb, chicken -is oven roasting. Put the meat on a rack in an open pan. Do not put seasoning on it, and do not cover. If the roast is not a particularly tender cut, it should roast for a long period at a low temperature.

STEAK BOBS

1 lb ribeye or NY steak
1 large onion
1 large bell pepper
1/2 lb small mushrooms

Cut steak, onion, and bell pepper into 1-inch pieces.
Precook onion and bell pepper 3 to 4 minutes on
HIGH in microwave. Alternate steak bites and
vegetables on skewers and broil to taste, either over
or under heat.
Turn skewers several times to cook evenly.

You can precook and assemble skewers ahead of
time and keep covered in the refrigerator until ready
to broil. Cherry tomatoes are also good on the bobs.

Serves 4.

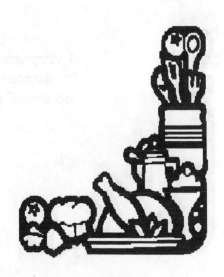

FAJITA SALAD

1 cup mild picante sauce or salsa
1 15-oz can pinto beans, drained
2 medium tomatoes, diced
1 ripe avocado, peeled, seeded & diced
1 lb sirloin or top round steak

Salt & pepper

OPTIONAL: Shredded lettuce and/or tortillas

Toss beans with 1/4 cup sauce; chill. Toss tomatoes and avocado with 1/4 cup sauce; chill. Salt and pepper meat to taste; broil to desired doneness. Slice thinly across grain. On a platter spread lettuce, if desired; arrange meat slices in center of platter, flanked by tomatoes and beans; scatter avocado on top. Spread remaining sauce over all. If desired, serve with tortillas and additional sauce or salsa. Serves 4.

A very attractive dish, which may be made ahead except for avocado. One neat trick is to scoop the avocado with the small end of a melon baller instead of dicing.

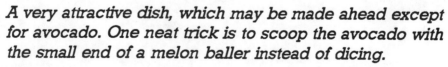

MEAT LOAF

1 1/2 lb ground lean beef
1 cup canned tomato sauce
3/4 cup quick oatmeal
1 egg, lightly beaten
1/2 onion, chopped

Salt & pepper to taste

Combine ingredients well but with a light hand for a nice texture. (Don't stir it to death.) Pack loosely into a greased or vegetable-cooking-sprayed loaf pan. Cook at 350° for 1 hour. Serves 4.

You can use ketchup to "ice" the loaf about 10 minutes before it is done and then sprinkle chopped parsley on it before serving. You can also substitute picante sauce for the tomato sauce if you like a spicier mix.

OVEN BAR-B-QUE

2 lbs round steak, cut in serving size pieces
1/4 cup flour
2 medium onions, sliced thin
1 cup Bulls Eye® bar-b-que sauce

2 TBS cooking oil
Salt & pepper

Dredge steak pieces with mixture of flour, salt and pepper. In Dutch oven on top of range, heat oil and brown steak over medium heat. Add bar-b-que sauce and simmer 5 minutes to concentrate liquid. Remove from heat, add onion slices. Cover and bake at 350⁰ for 1 hour, or until meat is fork tender.
Serves 4 or 5.

MUSTARD GRILLED STEAK

1/8 cup Dijon mustard
1/8 cup soy sauce
1 tsp dried thyme, crumbled
1 tsp minced fresh peeled ginger root
1 lb flank steaks

Pepper

Combine first 4 ingredients. Brush mixture over both sides of steaks, cover with plastic wrap and refrigerate for at least 6 hours or overnight. Grill or broil steaks on preheated grill to desired doneness; about 6 minutes on first side, 5 minutes on second side, for medium rare.
Slice diagonally across grain into thin slices (about 1/4-inch thick.) Serves 2.

BEEF FAJITAS

1 lb lean steak - flank, sirloin, tenderized
     round, chuck, etc.
1 medium onion, cut in 1/2 inch strips
1/2 green bell pepper, cut in 1/2 inch strips
1/2 red bell pepper, cut in 1/2 inch strips
4 flour or corn tortillas

Cooking oil
OPTIONAL: fresh salsa, or picante sauce

Steam tortillas over hot water, or put in warm oven, covered, to heat.
Broil steak and slice thinly across grain, then cut slices into 1/2 inch strips. Keep warm. Sauté onions and peppers in hot oil until tender, about 5 minutes. Arrange all ingredients on a platter for everyone to roll his own. Serve with salsa or picante sauce if you like. Serves 2 to 4.

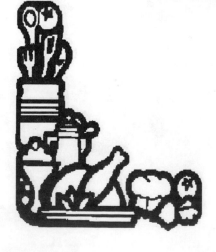

CHICKEN FRIED STEAK

2 minute (tenderized or cube) steaks
1 egg, beaten
4 TBS flour
1 cup milk

Salt & pepper
4 TBS oil

To 2 tablespoons of the flour, add salt and pepper to taste. Dip meat in egg, then dredge in flour mixture. Heat 2 tablespoons of the oil in a heavy skillet and fry meat till done, about 7 minutes on first side and 4 on second. Remove meat from skillet and keep warm. To drippings in skillet, add remaining 2 tablespoons oil and heat. Add remaining 2 tablespoons flour and brown, stirring constantly. Still stirring over medium heat, add milk. Cook and stir until desired consistency. Serves 2.

For a low-calorie gravy, shake together 2 tablespoons flour and 2 cups beef broth or beef boullion. Heat and cook 2 or 3 minutes; add salt and pepper to taste.

THE ORIGINAL BRISKET

1 whole beef brisket, untrimmed

Place brisket, fat side up (it must still have the fat on it, or you will have to lay pieces of suet where the fat should be) on a rack in a baking pan. Do not cover. Put pan in oven and turn oven to 250⁰. Bake 5 to 7 hours, or between noon and dinner time.
When you take the brisket out of the oven, trim fat from top and slice to serve. Serves a crowd.

The brisket doesn't need it, but if you wish, you can mix up a bar-b-que sauce to serve. Combine 1 cup burgundy, juice of 2 limes, 2 tablespoons Worcestershire sauce, 1 teaspoon liquid from jalapeños and 1 tablespoon liquid smoke.

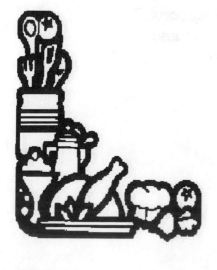

ISLETA CHILE BEEF

1 lb ground beef
1 lb potatoes, grated
1 4-oz can chopped green chile
1 small onion, chopped
4 medium-size fresh tomatoes, chopped

1 tsp salt

OPTIONAL; corn chips & grated cheese

Sauté meat over low to medium heat; drain. Add potatoes, onions, salt, chile and tomatoes, together with 2 cups water. Cover and simmer for 30 minutes. Transfer to a shallow baking dish, top with corn chips and grated cheese if desired. Bake at 325⁰ for 30 minutes.
Serves 4.

SWISS STEAK

1 lb steak, chuck or round
1 large onion, chopped
2 cloves garlic, minced
1 14-oz can tomatoes, undrained
1/2 cup dry white wine

Salt & pepper to taste
Cooking oil

Brown steak in oil in large skillet; remove from skillet, and sauté onion and garlic. Return steak to skillet. Cut up tomatoes if they are whole and add with liquid. Add wine. Cover and simmer on low heat for 1 hour. Serves 2 to 4.

BUDAPEST GOULASH

1 lb hamburger
1 16-oz can tomatoes
1 large onion, chopped
1 TBS paprika
4 oz home-style noodles, uncooked

1 TBS butter

In large heavy skillet, brown hamburger in butter, then add onions and cook until transparent. Do not drain.
Drain tomatoes, reserving juice. Add tomatoes and paprika to skillet mixture. (Chop tomatoes if they are whole.) Salt and pepper to taste. Cover, lower heat, and simmer 1 hour, stirring several times.
Add enough water to tomato liquid to make 2 cups and add to skillet. Raise heat to bring to boil.
Stir in noodles. Lower heat and gently boil, uncovered, for 30 minutes. Stir frequently as it may tend to stick.
Serves 4.

JANE'S HAMBURGER CASSEROLE

1 lb hamburger
1 large potato, peeled & thinly sliced
1 onion, chopped
1 16-oz can whole kernel corn, drained
1 16-oz can tomatoes, undrained

Salt & pepper

In a buttered 1-quart casserole, layer potato slices. Salt and pepper. Make layers of corn, onion, hamburger, and tomatoes, in that order, sprinkling each with salt and pepper. If tomato liquid does not reach halfway up the dish, add water.
Bake at 350° for 30 minutes covered; remove cover, bake another 30 minutes.
Serves 4-6.

HAMBURGER/GREEN BEANS

1 lb hamburger
2 cans cut green beans, undrained
1 onion, chopped
1 clove garlic, minced

Brown hamburger, onion, and garlic. Add green beans with liquid and simmer, covered, for 1 hour, adding water if necessary.
Serves 4-6.

Fresh green beans, left-over vegetables, other canned or frozen vegetables you happen to have will work with this formula. A dash of Worcestershire sauce may suit your taste more than, or in addition to, the garlic.

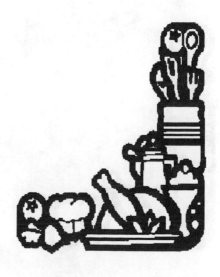

HAMBURGER/POTATOES

1 lb hamburger
1 cup instant mashed potatoes

Salt & Pepper to taste

OPTIONAL: 4-oz can chopped green chile, drained

Brown hamburger until done. Mix potatoes according to package directions. Add to hamburger, stir, and season. If desired, add green chile and stir in gently. Serves 4 to 6.

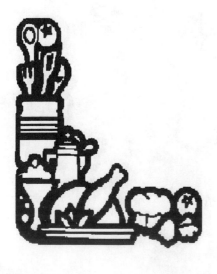

HAMBURGER PATTIES

1 lb hamburger
1 onion, chopped
1 egg, lightly beaten

Salt & Pepper to taste

Mix all ingredients and shape into 4 or 5 patties. Sauté over medium heat until done, about 7 minutes for first side, 3 minutes for second side.

You can omit the egg - it just helps hold the patty together.
Makes 4 or 5 hamburgers.

If you are cooking for children, of course, make 6 to 8 patties per pound of meat.

HAMBURGER MEXICAN

1 lb hamburger
2 cloves garlic, mashed
2 TBS chili powder

OPTIONAL: 1 onion, chopped

Brown hamburger partially. Add onion, if using, garlic and chili powder. Stir over medium heat until meat is done. Makes 4 to 6 tacos.

This is delicious as the filling meat for tacos, enchiladas, tostadas, whatever.

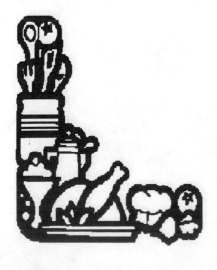

CHILI-CHIP PIE

1 6-oz pkg tortilla chips, broken
1 can cheddar cheese soup, undiluted
1 15-oz can chunky chili with beans

In the bottom of a lightly greased 1-quart baking dish, spread 2 cups of chip pieces. Layer half of soup over chips. Next, layer chili over soup; top with remaining soup. Bake, uncovered, at 350⁰ for 15 minutes; sprinkle with remaining chips and return to oven for 5 minutes. Serves 2 or 3.

Use Frito® brand chips for Frito® Pie.

A sure-fire success with kids, and other people, too.

SLOPPY JOES

1/2 lb hamburger
1/2 onion, chopped
1/4 cup ketchup, or to taste

2 buns, hotdog or hamburger style
Butter

Fry hamburger and onion in butter until done. Just before removing from the heat, stir in ketchup. Pile on buns and serve immediately.
Serves 2.

Anything with ketchup appeals to the younger generation. To go with Sloppy Joes you might heat a package of frozen French fries - and more ketchup.

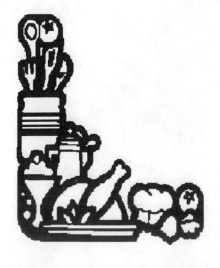

HAMBURGER/SPAGHETTI

1 lb hamburger
1 onion, chopped
1 clove garlic, mashed
1/4 tsp dried oregano
1 handful raw spaghetti, or 1 large can
    spaghetti

OPTIONAL: 1/2 cup grated cheese

In medium size skillet, brown hamburger, onion, and garlic. Stir in oregano. Meanwhile, cook spaghetti according to package directions, or open canned spaghetti. Combine, sprinkle with grated cheese if desired, and serve. Serves 4 to 6.

Now would be a good time to make garlic bread. Brush a combination of garlic salt and melted butter between slices of French bread, wrap in foil, and heat in 350° oven for 20 to 30 minutes. Then all you need is a simple green salad for a satisfying repast.

BEEF STRIPS IN SOUR CREAM

1 lb 1/2-thick round steak
1 onion, chopped
1 small can mushrooms
1/2 cup sour cream

2 TBS butter

Cut round steak in 1 inch strips. Brown in butter and remove. Brown onions in same butter. Put meat, onions, butter, mushrooms, sour cream, and 1/4 cup water in oven-proof dish. Bake, uncovered, at 350⁰ for 30 minutes. Serves 2 to 3.

You can serve this over cooked and buttered noodles and call it Beef Stroganoff!

MACARONI SAMANTHA

1 5-oz pkg Kraft® macaroni-cheese dinner
1/2 lb ground meat
1/2 medium onion, chopped
1 8-oz can tomato sauce

Salt & pepper

Cook macaroni according to package directions.
Brown the meat and onions. Add salt and pepper.
Drain macaroni and mix with meat, cheese package,
and tomato sauce. In a buttered casserole, cover and
bake at 350⁰ for 30 minutes.
Serves 2 to 3 adults or 4 to 6 children.

This is a little trouble, but so good it is worth it.
When the neighborhood children come to lunch, you will
be recognized as a great cook.

Use a large size macaroni-cheese dinner, 1 lb ground
meat and 15-oz can of tomato sauce for the next slumber
party.

TEX-MEX HOT DOGS

6 weiners
1 15-oz can Mexican-style beans
1 to 3 teaspoons chili powder
1 to 3 tablespoons fresh salsa or picante
    sauce
6 hot dog buns

Heat beans with chili powder and salsa. Grill weiners. Place split buns on grill to heat at the same time. Put an open bun on a plate, a hot dog on one side; top with beans. (You will need a fork or lots of paper napkins.) Serves 3 adults, 6 kids.

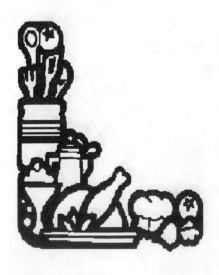

MEXICAN WEINERS

4 tortillas, corn or flour
4 weiners
4 tsp fresh salsa, or picante sauce
4 sticks cheddar cheese, 1/2"x1/8"x6"

Steam tortillas to heat, 1 or 2 minutes. Cook weiners on grill or in skillet. Place a weiner on a tortilla, spread with salsa, put cheese on top, and wrap in the hot tortilla.

On a cookout try this way: don't bother heating the tortillas; split the weiner almost through and insert the cheese stick before grilling.

GERMAN WEINERS

4 weiners
4 large cabbage leaves
4 sticks cheddar cheese, 1/2"x1/8"x6"
4 tsp pickle relish
4 tsp Dijon mustard

Steam cabbage leaves in microwave, about 4 minutes, covered. Split weiners, insert cheese sticks. Cover with pickle relish. Spread mustard along one side; wrap in cabbage leaf. Microwave, covered, at HIGH for 6 minutes or until thoroughly hot through.

Applesauce and hot cornbread round out the meal.

GUINNESS® POT ROAST

2-3 lb beef roast (chuck, shoulder)
1 bottle Guinness® stout
2 onions, finely chopped
2 TBS balsamic vinegar
1 cup pasta, in short lengths

1/2 tsp pepper
3 cups water

In a large heavy pot, brown beef. Add beer and pepper. Add onion and vinegar. Cover, lower heat and simmer 1 1/2 hours. Add 3 cups water, bring to boil and add pasta. Cook 20 to 30 minutes, or until pasta is done. Serves 4.

Also delicious with a pork roast.

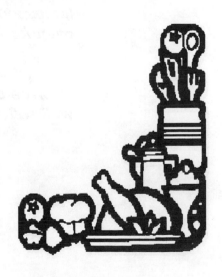

WINE PORK ROAST

3 to 4 lb pork loin
1/4 cup chopped onion
1 bay leaf
2 cups red wine
1 cup canned beef consommé

In heavy pot, brown loin on top of the stove. Add remaining ingredients. Bake uncovered at 350⁰ until done, about 2 hours, turning roast 2 or 3 times. Meat thermometer should read 170⁰. (Fresh pork is always cooked well done.)
Serves 4.

If you wish, add a cup of uncooked RICE (not instant) to the pan 20 minutes before the roast is finished. Cover and cook remaining time.

At the same time you may bake GLAZED ONIONS. Cut a slice from the bottoms of medium-sized onions so they will stand; discard outer shells and wrap individually in foil. After 1 hour or 1 1/2 hours, unwrap, put in baking dish, and pour over them a glaze of 1/4 cup butter, 2 tablespoons brown sugar and a dash of salt. Return to the oven for 20 to 30 minutes, basting several times.

In place of the rice, Oven Fried Potatoes (see recipe) go well with this. Allow 1 1/2 hours at 350⁰.

HAM & POTATO CASSEROLE

3 medium potatoes, unpeeled
1 cup milk
3 TBS flour
1 cup shredded cheddar cheese
8 or 10 slices boiled or baked ham

3 TBS butter
Salt & pepper to taste

Scrub potatoes and slice in 1/4 inch slices. Boil 10 minutes.
Meanwhile, make a white sauce. Melt butter in 2-cup measure in microwave (or in small skillet on top of stove.) Stir in flour until smooth. Add and stir milk. Microwave on high for 2 to 3 minutes, stirring after 1 1/2 minutes, (or cook and stir on top of stove) until thickened. Salt and pepper to taste.
In greased casserole, arrange single layer of potato slices. Sprinkle with 1/3 cup cheese. Cover with 4 or 5 thin slices of ham, overlapping slices slightly. Ladle small amount of white sauce over ham. Repeat layers, ending with potatoes and cheese.
Bake at 350^0, uncovered, 30 to 40 minutes.
Serves 6.

CHAMPAGNE HAM

1 fully cooked half ham, bone-in
3/4 cup champagne
1/3 cup Dijon mustard
3/4 cup brown sugar
1/4 cup brandy

Remove skin of ham and trim excess fat. Place on rack in roasting pan. Pour the champagne over ham. While cooking, baste frequently with pan drippings. Bake, uncovered, at 325⁰ for 20 to 22 minutes per pound. A meat thermometer inserted in thickest part of ham and not touching the bone, should register 140⁰.

While ham is baking, combine mustard, sugar and brandy. Cook and stir over low heat until sugar dissolves.
During last 30 minutes of baking ham, brush it several times with mustard mixture. A 6 to 8 lb ham will serve 12.

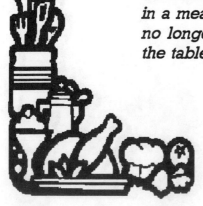

To remove a major source of stress in the kitchen, invest in a meat thermometer. It is perfectly simple to use, and no longer will you live in fear of putting a raw roast on the table.

BAKED HAM SLICE

2-inch-thick center cut ham slice
1 cup pineapple or orange juice
1/2 cup brown sugar

Score ham slice every 2 inches. Put in shallow baking dish and pour juice over. Sprinkle with sugar. Bake uncovered at 325⁰ for 1 1/2 to 2 hours, basting 2 or 3 times during baking. Serves 2.

For a meal that cooks itself while you spend an hour or two gardening or in the hammock: put 2 washed, unpeeled sweet potatoes in the oven to bake while the ham cooks; at the same time wash and core two large apples and set them upright in 1 inch of water in a small baking dish to cook along with ham and potatoes.

HAM ASPARAGUS ROLLS

6 spears fresh asparagus
1 TBS flour
1/4 tsp dry mustard
2 1-oz slices cooked ham
1/2 cup milk

1 TBS butter

OPTIONAL: 1/4 cup shredded Cheddar
cheese

Cook asparagus (see rule on page 197.)
Meanwhile, melt butter in a heavy pan over low heat.
Add flour and mustard and cook 1 minute, stirring
constantly. Add milk gradually, stirring and cooking
until mixture thickens.

On each slice of ham, put 3 asparagus spears, roll
and fasten with wooden toothpick. Arrange rolls in
baking dish; pour sauce over. Bake uncovered at 350⁰
for 20 minutes, or until thoroughly heated. Sprinkle
with cheese, if desired, and bake an additional 3 to 5
minutes. Serves 2.

GERMAN PORK CHOPS

4 thin (less than 1/2 in thick) pork chops,
    boned and trimmed
1/2 cup flour
2 eggs, beaten
1/4 cup milk
1 cup bread crumbs (or cornbread stuffing
    mix)

4 TBS butter
Salt & pepper

Mix flour with salt and pepper to taste; dredge chops.
Combine eggs and milk. Dip dredged chops in egg
mixture, then coat with crumbs. Sauté in hot butter
until done, about 8 minutes for first side, 3 minutes for
second side. Serves 2 to 4.

PORK CHOPS WITH APPLE SCHNAPPS

6 (1-inch or less) pork chops, trimmed
2 apples, quartered & sliced
3 TBS maple syrup
2 lemons
1/4 cup apple schnapps (apple brandy)

3 TBS butter

Grate rind of one lemon; squeeze both lemons for juice; set aside. Heat butter in pan, add apple slices, and cook quickly until lightly browned. Remove from pan. Add syrup and lemon juice - about 1/4 cup of lemon juice - to remaining butter in pan and stir. Add lemon rind and apple schnapps. Boil a few minutes until sauce thickens.
Grill chops, both sides, until cooked throughly. (Meat must be white or grayish all the way through, no trace of pink.) To serve, top chops with apple slices, then hot sauce.
Serves 6.

This sauce is also delicious on ham slices and even left-over slices of turkey or chicken.

PORK CHOPS WITH APPLES

4 pork chops, trimmed of fat
2 apples, cored & thickly sliced
2 cups half-and-half
Brown sugar

Salt & pepper to taste

Salt and pepper chops and brown on both sides over low to medium heat in large skillet. Arrange apple slices on chops. Sprinkle generously with brown sugar, covering meat and apples. Add half-and-half. Turn heat to low, cover tightly and cook until chops are done and apples soft, about 1 hour. Serves 4.

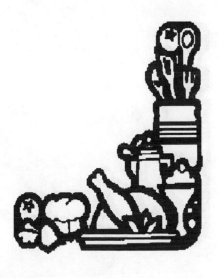

PORK CHOPS PATTY

4 pork chops, trimmed
1 egg, beaten
1 cup Pepperidge Farm® stuffing mix, crushed
1 cup dry sherry

Bacon grease or oil

Dip chops in egg and then dredge with crushed dressing mix. Brown both sides in bacon grease or oil over medium heat. Pour sherry over chops; lower heat, cover, and simmer until chops are done, about 45 minutes to an hour. Serves 2 to 4, depending on size of chops and appetites.

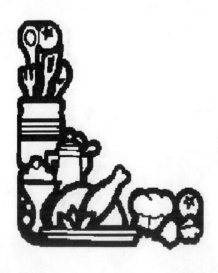

HAM-APRICOT LOAF

2 cups ground cooked ham
1 cup dry bread crumbs
1 cup ground dried apricots
1 cup milk
2 eggs, slightly beaten

Salt & Pepper

Combine ingredients and form into loaf. Bake uncovered at 300⁰ for 1 hour.

Loaf can be glazed with a fruit jam or preserves. Spread over loaf for last 10 minutes of cooking. Serves 4.

WILD PORK CHOPS

1 lb pork chops or trimmed pork steak
1/2 cup wild (and white) rice
1/2 green pepper, chopped
1/2 onion, chopped
1/2 can cream of chicken soup, undiluted

Salt & pepper
Butter

Brown pork in butter. Cook rice with onion and green pepper for 20 to 30 minutes, or according to directions on rice package (see note below). Mix chicken soup with rice mixture. In buttered casserole, put layer of half of vegetable mix, then pork chops, then rest of rice mixture.
Bake, uncovered, at 350⁰ for 45 minutes. If it seems to be getting too dry, add 1/4 cup water and cover for remaining cooking time.
Serves 4.

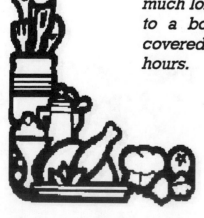

Wild rice alone is more flavorful than a combination of wild and white, but it is more expensive and requires much longer cooking. At high altitude, it must be brought to a boil, removed from heat, and allowed to soak, covered, for an hour before cooking an additional 1 1/2 hours.

LAMB PRIMAVERA

2 cups lamb steak, cut bite size
1 can tomatoes, undrained
1 onion, grated
1/4 green pepper, chopped
1 TBS A1® steak sauce

Butter
Salt & pepper

Brown lamb in butter. Mix with remaining ingredients and put in buttered casserole. Bake at 350⁰ for 45 minutes.
Serve over rice, or with mashed potatoes.
Serves 4.

This recipe works well with left-over lamb, too. Just omit browning, and proceed to mix and bake.

LAMB CURRY

2 cups lamb, diced
1 onion, diced
2 apples, diced
3/4 cup raisins
1 tsp curry powder, or to taste

1 TBS butter
OPTIONAL: flour to thicken liquid

Brown lamb and onion in butter. Add apples, raisins and seasoning. Cover and cook 10 minutes over medium-low heat. If desired, thicken liquid with 1 or 2 TBS flour dissolved in water and cook 5 minutes longer.

Serve over rice. Serves 4.

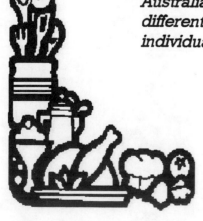

With any curry you may pass additional goodies to be sprinkled on top - shredded coconut, sliced almonds, chopped chives, dried banana slices, for example. In Australia they serve "13 Boy Curry", or curry with 13 different ingredients to be added by each guest to his individual taste.

SPICED LAMB CHOPS

4 rib or loin lamb chops, about 1 inch thick
2 cloves of garlic, mashed
2 tsp fresh parsley, chopped
1 tsp dried mint
1/2 tsp powdered ginger

Olive oil

Brush chops with oil on both sides and arrange in one layer in a shallow baking dish. Combine garlic, parsley, mint and ginger. Pat mixture onto top of chops.
Bake at 400° for 30 minutes.
Serves 4.

If you feel like using two handfuls, serve with Mint Wine Sauce.

The traditional lamb chop accompaniments are creamed potatoes and green peas, and it is a fool proof combination. Put a spoonful of mint jelly on the plate, too.

DEVILED LAMB SHANKS

3 lamb shanks
1/2 pkg (1.5-oz env.) onion soup mix

Plastic oven cooking bag

Shake envelope of mix to blend ingredients. Put mix and lamb shanks in cooking bag and turn several times to coat meat with seasoning. Add 2 tablespoons water. Close bag tightly and place in baking dish. Bake at 325^0 for 2 hours or until tender. Serves 2.

Beef works well with this recipe, too. It will tenderize a cheaper cut.

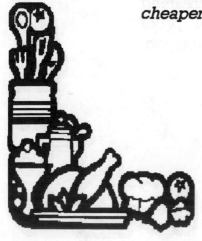

BANGERS AND CHOPS GRILL

PER PERSON

1 lamb chop
1 pork sausage link (or wiener)
1 garlic clove, mashed

Salt & pepper

Rub chops on each side with salt, pepper, and garlic. Heat grill and cook bangers (sausage links) and chops at the same time until done. Time depends on thickness of chops and heat of fire - perhaps 8 minutes on first side and 3 minutes on second.

An Australian favorite, this combination cooked on your grill is a delicious change from hamburgers! Any of the standards for a bar-b-que are good with it; try corn on the cob, and sliced tomatoes sprinkled with lemon-pepper and basil.

ORIENTAL LAMB

2 lbs lamb steak, cut in serving pieces
1 cup white wine
1 clove garlic, minced
1 TBS soy sauce
1/4 tsp ground ginger

Salt & pepper

Combine wine, garlic, soy sauce and ginger. Marinate lamb for 1 or 2 hours, turning occasionally. Broil or grill to desired degree. Salt and pepper to taste.
Serves 4.

Rice would be appropriate and delicious. Toss a generous handful of chopped parsley with the cooked rice for color and flavor, or try Raisin Nut Rice.

ROAST LEG OF LAMB

4 to 6 lb leg of lamb
3 garlic cloves, sliced

1 TBS flour

Make a half dozen small slits in roast and insert slices of garlic. Roast at 475⁰ for 30 minutes. Reduce heat to 325⁰ and continue roasting, allowing 20 minutes per pound until internal temperature reaches 175⁰. Baste occasionally, and just before it is ready to be taken out, season with salt and pepper. Remove from pan and keep warm.

For gravy: pour off all but 2 tablespoons of fat in pan. Add 1 1/2 cups hot water and scrape up browned bits. Mix flour with a little cold water and whisk in to thicken. Bring to boiling point, season with salt and pepper. Strain, if necessary, to remove lumps (though a whisk should smooth them out, and the brown bits are tasty.)

Accompany the lamb roast with canned peach halves filled with Major Grey's chutney amd baked at 300⁰ for 30 minutes, or at 325⁰ for the last 20 minutes of the lamb roasting.

KATE'S COLA CHICKEN

4 chicken breasts or thighs
1 cup Coca Cola®
1 cup ketchup
1/4 cup finely chopped onion

Put chicken in baking dish. Mix remaining ingredients and pour over. Cover and bake at 325⁰ for 2 hours. Serves 2 to 4.

If you have a slow cooker, you can put the chicken and sauce in it in the morning and have a wonderful meal when you get home after work.

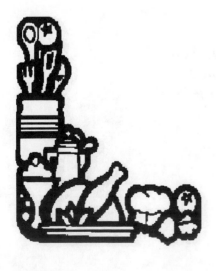

CHICKEN & HAM ALMONDINE

1 can cream of mushroom soup, undiluted
1 cup cooked diced chicken
1/2 cup slivered toasted almonds
4 thin slices ham (or 1 can deviled ham)
4 halves English muffin, buttered & toasted

Mix soup, chicken, and almonds and heat over medium heat. Place slice of ham on each muffin half, or spread with deviled ham. Spoon hot chicken mixture over.
Serves four (lightly).

Pair this with a fruit salad for a light luncheon or supper.

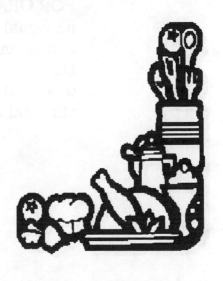

SOUTHERN FRIED CHICKEN

1 frying chicken, cut up
2 cups flour
1 TBS baking powder
1 TBS poultry seasoning
1/2 can evaporated milk (for gravy)

Salt & pepper
Cooking oil for frying

Soak chicken 1 hour in lightly salted water.
Combine baking powder, poultry seasoning, salt and pepper with flour. Dredge chicken pieces. (Put flour mixture in paper bag and shake pieces one at a time.)
Reserve flour mixture.
In a deep heavy skillet, heat 3/4 inch deep oil. Fry one layer of chicken pieces, skin side up, for 12 to 15 minutes. Turn and fry 2 or 3 minutes. Remove to hot platter and keep warm while you fry remaining chicken. Serves 4.

FOR GRAVY; Drain pan drippings leaving 3 TBS. Add an equal amount of reserved seasoned flour mixture. Brown the flour in the drippings over medium heat, stirring constantly. Still stirring, add 1/2 can evaporated milk mixed with 1/2 can water. Cook and stir until desired consistency.

BAKED CHICKEN & RICE

1/4 cup onion, chopped
1 cup cooked (or canned) chicken, cut up
2 cups chicken broth
1 cup shredded Velveeta® cheese
1/2 cup regular rice (not instant)

1 TBS butter

Sauté onion in butter until transparent.   Add
remaining ingredients. Put in 1 1/2 quart casserole.
Cover and bake at 375⁰ for 1 hour. Serves 2.

CHICKEN FRICCASSEE

4 halves chicken breasts or whole thighs,
    skinned and boned
1 10-oz can cream of chicken soup,
    undiluted
1 1/3 cups dry white wine
1 6-oz pkg long-grain & wild rice

Vegetable cooking spray

Cook rice according to package directions (see note on wild rice on page 122.)
In a large skillet coated with cooking spray, brown chicken on both sides over medium heat. Remove chicken from pan. Combine soup and wine in the skillet and heat to boiling. Stir in cooked rice. Place chicken on rice. Cover, lower heat, and simmer until chicken is done (juices run clear when pierced deeply with fork), about 1/2 hour. Serves 4.

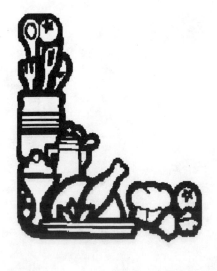

CHICKEN BURGUNDY

2 1/2 lb fryer, cut up
1/2 cup flour
4 slices bacon
1 cup chopped onions (or green onions)
1 cup burgundy or other dry red wine

1 tsp salt
1/4 tsp pepper

OPTIONAL: 8-oz fresh mushrooms, sliced

Mix flour, salt and pepper; dredge chicken pieces in mixture. In a heavy pot or Dutch oven, fry bacon until crisp; remove to drain. Brown chicken in bacon grease. Remove and set aside. Add onions to pot, and mushrooms if desired, and cook until tender. Crumble bacon and stir into onions (and mushrooms); add chicken and remaining ingredients with 1 cup water. Cover and simmer until chicken is done, about 35 minutes. Serves 4.

CHICKEN MEDITERRANEAN

4 halves chicken breasts or whole thighs,
    skinned
1 large onion, finely chopped
2 14-oz cans whole plum tomatoes, undrained
2 cloves garlic, mashed
1 tsp Italian seasoning, or fines herbes

Salt & pepper to taste
OPTIONAL: 1/4 cup grated Parmesan cheese

Place all ingredients except cheese in Dutch oven or large skillet. Bring to boil, lower heat, cover and simmer 45 minutes or until chicken is done (juices run clear when meat is pierced deeply with fork.) Sprinkle with cheese if desired and serve. Serves 4.

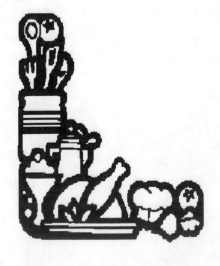

CHICKEN MERELYN

6 chicken thighs or 1 cut-up chicken, skinned
Garlic salt
1/2 cup flour
Tarragon or rosemary
1 cup white wine

Butter

Sprinkle both sides of skinned chicken pieces with garlic salt; dredge generously with flour. Place fleshy side up in shallow, oven-proof buttered pan, in one layer only. Sprinkle top of each piece with tarragon or rosemary.
Bake, uncovered, 40 minutes at 350^0; then baste with white wine, dampening all the flour. Bake another 20 to 30 minutes. Serves 4 to 6.

Nothing could be simpler or better. When you are out of ideas, this is always easy and good.

CHICKEN ORANGE

6 chicken breasts, skinned
1 pkg onion soup mix
1 small can frozen orange juice, undiluted
1 fresh orange, peeled, sliced, seeded

Butter

Place chicken, fleshy side up, in buttered shallow baking dish. Sprinkle with soup mix. Spoon orange juice on top of chicken. Arrange orange slices on top. Cover with foil and bake at 350° for 1 hour and 15 minutes; remove foil and bake 15 minutes longer. Serves 6.

When your oven is going to be on for an hour, why not put in a vegetable dish such as Corn Bake or Oven-Baked Vegetables to cook at the same time?

APRICOT CHICKEN

1 frying chicken, whole or cut up
1 bottle Russian dressing
1 small jar apricot preserves
1 pkg onion soup mix

Put chicken in deep oven dish. Mix remaining ingredients and pour over chicken. Cover and bake at 350⁰ for 2 hours or more.
Serves 2 to 4.

Another recipe for a slow cooker, start the chicken and sauce before you go to work (or play) and have supper ready when you get home.

CHICKEN ITALIANO

1 2 to 3 lb frying chicken, skinned & cut up
1 cup Italian salad dressing
1 pkg onion soup mix
1/2 tsp oregano
Crushed bran flakes

Mix oregano into soup mix. Dip chicken pieces in Italian dressing; dredge in onion soup mix, then in bran flakes. In a greased shallow baking dish, bake uncovered at 350^0 for 1 hour and 15 minutes. Serves 2 to 4.

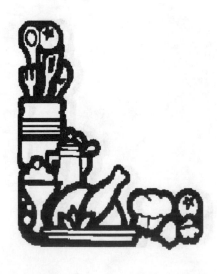

KATHY'S GREEN CHILE CHICKEN

1 whole fryer chicken
1 can cream of chicken soup, undiluted
1 can cheddar cheese soup, undiluted
1/2 cup chopped hot green chiles
6 corn tortillas

OPTIONAL: 1/2 cup grated cheddar
   cheese

Boil chicken, remove meat from bones and shred. It should make 3 to 4 cups of shredded meat. Combine soups. Add chicken and green chile. Cook, stirring, over medium heat until hot. Tear tortillas into bite-sized pieces and layer 1/2 of pieces in bottom of buttered shallow baking dish. Spoon 1/2 of chicken mixture over tortillas, then layer remaining tortillas. Top with remaining chicken mixture. If desired, sprinkle with grated cheese. Bake uncovered at 350⁰ for about 25 minutes. Serves 4 to 6.

All you need with this dish is a green salad or sliced tomatoes, but you might also serve refried beans or other canned beans if you are having more people. Beer, especially Mexican beer, goes naturally with New Mexican food.

CHICKEN APPLE SALAD

2 cups cold cooked chicken
1 1/2 cups cold cooked brown rice
1 large red apple, diced
1 cup Miracle Whip®
1 cup chopped jicama or celery

Combine ingredients and chill at least an hour, to meld flavors. Serves 4.

If you sprinkle the cut apple with lemon juice it prevents its turning brown.

Served on a lettuce leaf, and accompanied by Date Muffins, Corn Biscuit Fingers, or another hot bread, this is a delightful luncheon dish.

OVEN CHICKEN FINGERS

1 cup crushed flake cereal
1/2 cup buttermilk (or yogurt)
1/2 tsp fines herbes
1/2 tsp garlic powder
6 halves chicken breasts or whole thighs,
    boned, skinned

Vegetable cooking spray

Cut chicken into 1-inch wide strips. Combine buttermilk or yogurt with seasonings. Dip each chicken strip into mixture; coat with cereal crumbs. Place on baking sheet coated with cooking spray. Bake at 350⁰ for 18 minutes; turn and bake an additional 15 minutes or until golden. Serves 6.

You could team Chicken Fingers with Parmesan Potato Sticks. Children especially like finger food.

CHICKEN SALAD

2 cups cooked chicken, cut up
1 cup chopped celery
1 cup green grapes, halved
1/4 cup sliced almonds
1 cup mayonaisse

Salt & pepper

OPTIONAL: 1/4 cup sliced water chestnuts

Combine and chill for 2 hours or more. Serves 4.

If you add 2 tablespoons soy sauce and 1 tablespoon curry to the mayonaisse, it makes a spicy change. You may substitute chopped pecans for the almonds.

This recipe also makes a successful tunafish salad. Simply substitute a small can of tuna for the chicken, and add 1 teaspoon mustard to the mayonaisse.

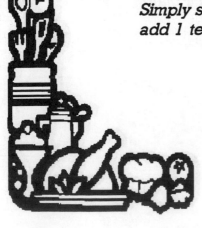

DUCK L'ORANGE

1 4-to-6 lb duck, fresh or frozen (thawed)
1 orange
1 lemon, juiced
2 TBS Curacao liqueur
1 1/2 tsp cornstarch

Peel zest (thin yellow rind) from orange, and put zest in freezer for 30 minutes. Squeeze orange, reserving juice, squeezed rind and pulp.

Preheat oven to 450⁰.
Put squeezed orange peel and pulp in duck cavity. Place duck on rack in roasting pan, uncovered. Put in oven and lower heat to 350⁰. Roast until tender, about 20 minutes per pound, basting with pan juices several times. Remove duck to a hot platter, discard orange peel and pulp, and cover with foil to keep warm. Drain grease from roasting pan, but leave brown bits.

Shred frozen zest in processor or mince with sharp knife. Heat reserved orange juice (with enough water to make 1 cup) in roasting pan, scraping up brown bits. Add zest, lemon juice, Curacao, and cornstarch, stirring constantly. Stir and cook a few minutes until sauce is moderately thickened. Serve immediately over already carved duck meat or, if you carve at the table, pass in a sauceboat. Serves 4-6.

TURKEY & DRESSING

1 10-to-14 lb turkey
1 loaf day-old white bread
1 large onion, chopped
2 apples, unpeeled, cored & chopped
1 whole stalk celery, chopped

Salt & pepper

Preheat oven to 450°. Remove giblets from turkey and put in a saucepan to simmer in 2 cups water for 30 minutes to 1 hour. Put turkey on rack in roasting pan. Take a long piece of foil, tuck it in the handle of pan at one end, reach over the bird and tuck into the handle on the other end, forming a tent open at the sides. Put the turkey in the oven and lower the heat to 350°. Cook until done, about 15 to 20 minutes per pound, depending on size. A meat thermometer inserted in meat of thigh (not touching bone) should read 180°-185°.

DRESSING: Tear bread into 1" pieces. Combine with onion, apples, celery, and season generously with salt and pepper. Drain giblets, reserving cooking liquid. Dice giblets and add to dressing along with liquid. If dressing is not moist enough, add water. Put dressing in buttered shallow baking dish and bake uncovered at 350° for 45 minutes to 1 hour. When it is crusty on top but before it is too dry, remove from oven and cover to keep warm.

If you stuff your bird with dressing add 5 minutes per pound in cooking and do not leave stuffing in the left-over turkey; remove and refrigerate separately.

HOT (PICANTE) MARINADE FOR PORK OR CHICKEN

1/4 cup burgundy
1/4 cup Worcestershire sauce
1/8 cup soy sauce
1/8 cup olive oil
Tabasco® to taste

Combine ingredients. You might start with 3 dashes of Tabasco® and taste for heat. You can always add more.
Marinate meat (up to 1 1/2 lbs of pork or chicken) for 3 to 4 hours, turning every hour.
Remove meat, reserving marinade. While you broil chops or chicken, cook the marinade down to 1/2 its volume to make a sauce. Pour sauce over and serve. If you use 1 1/2 lbs meat, it will serve 3-4.

An easy and efficient way to marinate meat is to put meat and marinade in a sturdy plastic bag, like a cooking plastic bag, close tightly and chill in the refrigerator, turning the bag over every half hour or so.

SPICY PLUM SAUCE

2 10-oz jars plum jam or preserves
2 TBS dry white wine or fresh lemon juice
1 tsp cinnamon
1/2 tsp powdered ginger
1/4 tsp ground cloves

In a small saucepan, heat jam over medium heat, stirring occasionally, until melted, 2 to 3 minutes. Add remaining ingredients and stir to blend well. Simmer 2 minutes. If using as a glaze, let cool slightly before brushing over meat. Makes about 2 1/2 cups.

This is excellent with ham or pork chops; if used with broiled chicken it gives an oriental touch.

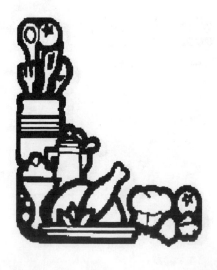

MINT WINE SAUCE

1/4 cup dry red wine
2 TBS confectioner's sugar
1/3 cup red wine vinegar
Zest (thin rind) of 1 orange, finely grated
3 TBS chopped fresh mint (3 tsp dried)

1/8 tsp pepper

In a small saucepan heat wine with sugar: stir to dissolve sugar. Remove to bowl and add vinegar. After blanching orange zest in boiling water for 15 seconds, add it to vinegar mixture. Stir in mint and pepper. Chill at least 1 hour. Yield: about 1/2 cup.

The sauce may be spooned over lamb chops, pork chops, ham slices, or used as a salad dressing.
Try it with a fruit salad, for example.

CRANBERRY SAUCE

2 cups cranberries
1 cup sugar
1 cup water

Pick over and wash cranberries. Boil sugar and water together for 5 minutes. Add cranberries. Lower heat and simmer gently, uncovered, without stirring for 5 minutes or until berries are transparent. Rinse mold in cold water and pour in sauce. Chill.

CRANBERRY RELISH

2 cups cranberries
1 whole orange
1 cup sugar

Scrub orange, cut in pieces and remove seeds. Pick over and wash cranberries. Put all ingredients in processor and process until a coarse relish consistency. Chill overnight.

For a change, add 1 teaspoon of cinnamon and 1/2 teaspoon cloves to either of the above sauces.

VEGETABLES

Many garden-fresh vegetables - broccoli, green beans, asparagus, spinach, peas, squash - retain the best flavor (and their vitamins) if cooked the basic way. Steam them, covered, in a small amount of water, until tender. Dressing should be simple; mayonaisse with a little lemon juice or mustard added, or just butter, salt and pepper.

Tender new potatoes in their jackets, or fresh young corn-on-the-cob are marvelous when boiled just til done. Add a cup of milk to water for the corn.

The (only slightly) more complicated recipes in the following section are for those times when the produce is not perfect and needs a little help, or when you have an inclination for something different.

ASPARAGUS WITH MUSHROOMS

3 cups cut asparagus, freshly cooked
1 cup fresh or canned mushrooms, sliced
1/2 cup cream
1 TBS chopped green onions

1/4 cup butter

If mushrooms are fresh, sauté them in additional butter for 2 to 3 minutes and remove from pan. Sauté onion and asparagus in the 1/4 cup butter for 5 minutes. Add mushrooms and cream and heat to very hot before serving. Serves 4 to 6.

An especially good dish to serve with ham, it can be a real short cut with frozen asparagus and canned mushrooms. Canned asparagus is possible, though not as good.

ASPARAGUS WITH DILL VINAIGRETTE

3/4 lb asparagus, trimmed
1 egg, hard-cooked, peeled, halved
1 TBS fresh lemon juice
1 TBS minced fresh dill
1 TBS drained capers

2 TBS olive oil
Salt & pepper

Cook asparagus until crisp-tender (see rule page 197); drain and cool.
Separate egg yolk and white. Mince egg white, set aside. Mash yolk with lemon juice and slowly add oil. Add dill, capers, salt and pepper.
To serve, arrange asparagus on plates, spoon vinaigrette over. Sprinkle with minced egg white. Serves 2 to 3.

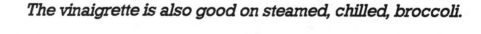

The vinaigrette is also good on steamed, chilled, broccoli.

BACON CORN

2 cups whole kernel corn, uncooked
4 slices bacon
1 TBS sugar
1/2 cup milk

Salt & pepper

Fry bacon or microwave until crisp. Crumble bacon. Combine all ingredients with salt and pepper to taste, and put in 1-quart baking dish. Bake, covered, at 350⁰, for 30 minutes. Serves 4.

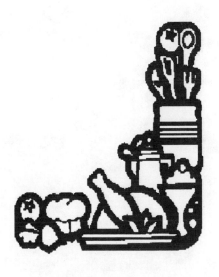

CORN BAKE

1 cup biscuit mix
1 15-oz can creamed corn
1 egg, lightly beaten
1 cup canned Italian-style tomatoes
4 oz grated cheese

2 TBS butter

Combine mix, corn, egg, tomatoes, butter and 2 oz of the cheese. Add 1/4 cup water. Mix lightly but thoroughly. Put in greased shallow baking dish, 8" x 8". Spread remaining cheese on top. Bake at 350⁰ for 30 to 40 minutes, or until table knife inserted in center comes out clean. Serves 4 to 6.

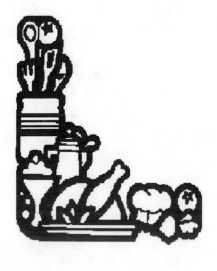

CHILE CORN

2 cups frozen corn
1 4-oz can chopped mild green chile

1/2 tsp butter
1/2 cup water
Salt & pepper

Combine and microwave on HIGH for 5 minutes, stirring after 2 minutes. Or, combine and cook on top of stove according to package directions for corn.

You can sprinkle grated cheese on top if you like, but it is delicious without it. Serves 4.

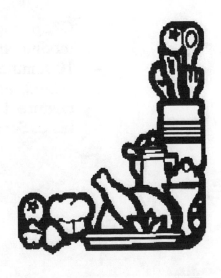

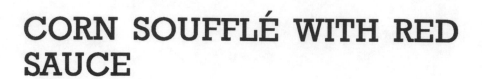

CORN SOUFFLÉ WITH RED SAUCE

1 7-oz can whole kernel corn
2 TBS flour
3 eggs, separated
Small amount of milk
2 TBS butter

Drain corn, reserving liquid. Stir flour into melted butter and cook for 1 minute. Add enough milk to reserved corn liquid to make 3/4 cup. Whisk into butter and flour, and cook until thickened. Add egg yolks one at a time. Stir in corn. Salt and pepper to taste. Beat egg whites until stiff. Stir small amount into corn mixture; fold in remaining egg whites. In a buttered soufflé dish, bake at 375° for 1 hour. Serves 2.

RED BELL & TOMATO SAUCE

2 large red bell peppers, seeded
2 large tomatoes, chopped
1 TBS butter

Chop peppers into 1" pieces and sauté in butter over medium heat until tender, stirring several times, for about 10 minutes. In processor, puree until smooth. Return to skillet; add tomatoes. Cook over medium heat until mixture is thick, about 20 minutes. Salt and pepper to taste. Serve over or under soufflé.

CALABACITAS

1 onion, chopped
1 clove garlic, mashed
3 small zucchini and/or yellow squash, sliced
1 small can whole kernel corn
1 small can chopped mild green chile,
    undrained

Butter

OPTIONAL: 1 cup grated cheese

Melt 2 pats butter in large frying pan on top of stove.
Sauté onion and garlic about 5 minutes. Add squash
to pan and continue cooking for about 10 minutes.
Add corn, drained, and chile with liquid. Cook until
heated through, but don't let squash get soggy.
Remove from heat and, if desired, stir in cheese
before serving. Serves 4.

CREAMY CALABACITAS

1 lb squash, zucchini and/or yellow
4 oz cream cheese, room temperature
1 8-oz can whole kernel corn, drained
1/2 cup milk
1 cup green chile, mild, chopped

Salt & pepper

Slice squash, add water and simmer until medium soft; drain. Add milk, cream cheese, corn, and chile. Cook over medium heat, stirring continually, until hot, smooth and thickened.
Serves 4.

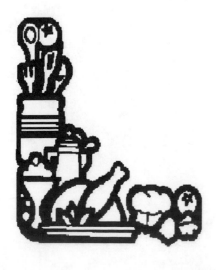

OVEN-BAKED VEGETABLES

1 onion, chopped
1 stalk broccoli, in florets
2 medium tomatoes, thin sliced
Lemon pepper (or salt & pepper)
1/4 cup buttered crumbs

Butter

Sauté onion in butter in small skillet. Add broccoli. Cover, but stir often so onion does not burn. When onion is tender, transfer it and broccoli to buttered pie pan. Sprinkle with lemon pepper. Top with slices of tomato, lemon pepper. Cover with foil; bake 350° for 30 minutes.
Sprinkle top with buttered crumbs, bake uncovered another 10 minutes. Serves 2.

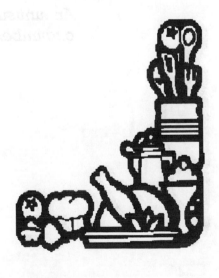

CUCUMBERS IN CHEESE SAUCE

2 or 3 medium cucumbers, peeled & sliced
1 can condensed cheddar cheese soup,
     undiluted

Salt & pepper

Cook cucumber slices in boiling salted water until tender, about 15 minutes. Heat cheese soup; do not add water. Drain cooked cucumbers and stir soup in carefully. Salt and pepper to taste. Serves 4.

An unusual vegetable dish using the always available cucumber.

POSOLE

2 lbs fresh lean pork, cut up
2 lbs hominy
2 onions, diced
3 TBS ground chili powder
3 cloves garlic, minced

Salt & pepper

In large heavy pot, combine all ingredients; add water to cover. Bring to boil; cover, lower heat and simmer 2 to 2 1/2 hours, the longer the better. You will have to add water as it is needed. Add more chili powder (or Tabasco® sauce) if you want it hotter. Serves a crowd.

A New Mexican dish, posole is not only good with green chile stew, but with brisket or bar-b-que or any other hearty meat.

ROUNDUP BEANS

1 lb dry beans (pinto, navy)
2 onions, chopped
4 cloves garlic, minced
1 ham bone or 2 ham hocks

Soak dry beans overnight in water to cover. Add onion, garlic and ham bone. Bring to boil, cover, lower heat. Cook until beans are done. Cooking time may vary from 2 to 12 hours, depending on altitude and taste. You will need to add water as beans cook and absorb it. Serves a crowd.

Among the additions you can make to beans are broccoli stalks-peeled, sliced, and pre-cooked till tender. Puree them and add with liquid to the beans.

CARIBBEAN BLACK BEANS

1 lb black beans
1 lemon, thinly sliced
2 cloves garlic, mashed
2 large onions, chopped
1/2 lb ham, cut in 1" cubes

Salt & pepper

Soak beans for 12 hours in water to cover. (At a high altitude you need to use a pressure cooker.) Start cooking the beans in the morning; add lemon slices, garlic, and ham: cook all day, adding water as needed. Serves a crowd.

The traditional, and most delicious, way to serve black beans is over cooked white rice. As an added fillip, for each person split a ripe banana lengthwise and sauté it in butter on both sides till golden - an island treat.

BAKED BEANS

2 15-oz cans pork & beans, drained
1/2 cup molasses
1 small onion, finely chopped
1 green bell pepper, finely chopped
6 slices bacon, uncooked

Mix beans with molasses, onion, and pepper.
Spread in lightly greased 9" x 13" baking dish.
Arrange bacon slices on top. Bake, covered, at 350⁰
for 30 minutes; then remove cover and bake about 30
minutes longer, or until bacon is done. Do not allow
to overcook and dry out. (You can keep it warm
covered with foil in a warm oven.) Serves 10 or more.

Nothing is better for a gathering than brisket and baked beans.

MINTED GLAZED CARROTS

1 16-oz can small carrots, drained
1/2 cup sugar
2 TBS chopped fresh mint (1/2 TBS dried)

1/4 cup butter

Melt sugar and butter till sugar dissolves. Add carrots. Stir gently to coat and cook over low heat until glazed but not brown. Sprinkle with mint just before serving. Serves 6.

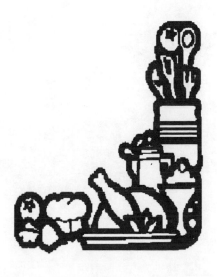

SWEET SPICY CARROTS

1 1/2 lb. young carrots
1/4 cup brown sugar
1 1/2 TBS chopped chives
1 1/2 tsp dry mustard

1/2 cup butter
Salt & pepper

Wash, peel, and cut carrots into 3" x 1/2" sticks. Sauté in butter over medium heat for 5 minutes. Add remaining ingredients. Reduce heat, cover, and cook for 10 minutes or until tender. Serves 6 to 8.

EGGPLANT PARMESAN

2 small eggplants
1 cup Italian bread crumbs
1 14-oz jar Ragu Spaghetti Sauce®
1/4 cup freshly grated Parmesan cheese

Olive oil

Slice eggplant in 1/4" slices. Dip in water and dredge in breadcrumbs. Sauté in oil over medium-low heat for 10 minutes per side. Layer in buttered casserole as follows: on the bottom, 2 tablespoons of spaghetti sauce; eggplant slices, overlapped; 1/3 of remaining sauce; 1/3 cheese. Repeat, ending with cheese. Bake at 350⁰ for 30 to 45 minutes. Serves 6 to 8.

The recipe can be cut in half, and it also makes a very good zucchini dish.

BROCCOLI WITH SESAME SEEDS

1 TBS sesame seeds
1 lb broccoli, cut into florets
1/2 tsp soy sauce
1 tsp white wine vinegar

1 1/2 tsp oil

Toss broccoli with oil and sesame seeds. Put in microwave-proof dish, cover, and microwave on HIGH for 4 minutes. (OR steam broccoli until tender, then add other ingredients.) Add soy and vinegar and toss to coat. Serves 4.

WILD BROCCOLI

1/2 cup wild rice, uncooked
2 cups fresh or frozen broccoli, chopped
1 cup celery, chopped
1/2 can condensed cheddar cheese soup

Salt & pepper

OPTIONAL; 1 clove garlic, mashed

Cook rice according to package directions.*
Meanwhile, cook broccoli and celery together, either
in microwave or saucepan. Place cooked rice in
buttered casserole. Cover with vegetables, combined
with garlic if desired. Salt and pepper to taste. Dilute
cheese soup and pour over. Cover and bake at 350⁰
for 30 minutes. You may remove cover for last ten
minutes if you like a drier topping.
Serves 4 to 6.

*See note on wild rice on page 122.

CORN-BROCCOLI BAKE

1 10-oz pkg frozen chopped broccoli, thawed
1 16-oz can creamed corn
1/2 cup saltine cracker crumbs
1 egg, beaten
1/2 cup onion, finely chopped

4 TBS butter, melted
Salt & pepper

Combine broccoli, corn, egg, onion, half of the cracker crumbs and half of the butter. Salt and pepper to taste. Place in buttered 1-quart baking dish. Mix remaining crumbs and butter and sprinkle on top. Cover, and bake at 350⁰ for 45 minutes. Serves 4-6.

SALSA STUFFED ZUCCHINI BOATS-MICROWAVE

2 small zucchini, cut in half lengthwise
1/2 small onion, finely chopped
1/2 cup mild fresh salsa
2/3 cup low-fat cottage cheese
2 oz Monterey Jack cheese, grated

Scoop out each zucchini half, leaving a 1/4-inch shell. Discard pulp. Place zucchini cut side down in baking dish. Cover and microwave on HIGH for 2 to 4 minutes, until tender but not limp. Drain, and turn cut sides up.
Combine onion with salsa and microwave on HIGH 3 to 4 minutes, stirring once. Stir in cottage cheese. Spoon mixture into zucchini shells, rounding tops. Sprinkle grated cheese on tops. Microwave on MEDIUM for 5 or 6 minutes, or until cheese is melted. Serves 2.

Like most recipes, this can be made without a microwave. Boil the zucchini and sauté the onion on top of the stove, and run the stuffed boats under the broiler to finish.

ZUCCHINI PARMESAN

6 small zucchini
1/2 small onion, thinly sliced
2 medium tomatoes, thinly sliced
1/4 cup Parmesan cheese

4 TBS olive oil
Salt & pepper

Wash, and cut zucchini into about 1/2 inch slices. Cook in boiling salted water until tender, or microwave. Drain. Sauté onion in olive oil until yellow. In a buttered casserole, put a layer of zucchini, then sliced tomatoes, then onion. Sprinkle with salt and pepper, then half the cheese. Repeat layers. Bake at 375⁰ for 30 minutes. Serves 6.

If you like a more Italian flavor, add 1/2 teaspoon of oregano sprinkled on each layer. This recipe works with eggplant, also.

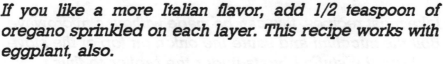

HOT ZUCCHINI

3 small zucchini, sliced
3 slices bacon
1/2 can Rotel® tomatoes & chilies
1 can cream of mushroom soup, undiluted
2 to 3 oz grated cheese

Fry or microwave bacon until crisp. Drain and crumble. Combine first four ingredients. Put in a buttered 1-quart baking dish. Bake uncovered at 350^0 for 20 minutes; sprinkle top with cheese, bake another 10 minutes. Serves 4.

NEW MEXICAN RICE

2 1/2 cups cooked rice
1 8-oz pkg cream cheese, softened
1 4-oz can chopped mild green chile
1/2 lb Monterey Jack cheese, grated
1 TBS oregano

Combine all ingredients, reserving 1/4 cup cheese. Place in buttered 2-quart casserole and sprinkle reserved cheese on top. Bake at 350⁰ for 30 minutes. Serves 6.

For a milder dish, substitute a can of chopped pimientos for the green chile.

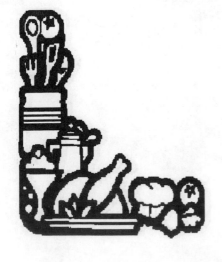

RED & GREEN RICE

2 cups chicken broth
1 cup uncooked brown rice
1 red bell pepper, chopped
1/2 cup chopped green onions
1 can mushrooms (or 6 fresh, sliced)

OPTIONAL: 1 jalapeño pepper, chopped

Simmer rice, covered, in chicken broth until tender. At high altitude brown rice may require an hour or more, like wild rice. (See note on wild rice, page 122.) Add remaining ingredients and put in baking dish. Bake covered at 350⁰ for 1 hour.
Serves 6.

RAISIN NUT RICE

2 cups instant rice
1/2 cup raisins
1/3 cup chopped pecans or almonds
1/3 cup milk

1 TBS butter

Cover raisins with boiling water and let soak for 1/2 to 1 hour. Separately, cover nuts with milk to soak for same time.
Cook rice according to package directions.
Drain raisins and nuts, add to rice along with butter, and toss gently. Serves 4.

FRENCH CARAMEL ONIONS

3 medium onions, thinly sliced
1 TBS brown sugar
2 TBS red wine vinegar
4 small hard rolls

3 TBS olive oil
Salt & pepper

In a heavy skillet heat oil. Add onions and cook over low heat about 30 minutes until they begin to brown. Add sugar, vinegar, salt and pepper. Cook 5 more minutes.
Slice off tops of rolls and remove centers.
Divide onions into rolls; replace tops if you choose before serving. Serves 4.

Whenever you sauté or fry, always have oil hot before you add anything; the food will absorb much less fat and be tastier and crisper, not to mention healthier.

STUFFED ONIONS

4 large white onions, whole
1 cup ground cooked beef or pork
1/4 cup chopped chives
1/2 cup grated Haverti cheese

Remove outside skin and cut a 1/2" slice off each onion. In boiling water to cover, simmer onions for 30 minutes. Drain. When cool enough to handle, scoop out centers, leaving a 1/2" wall. Combine meat with chives and 1/4 cup cheese. If you need it for volume, chop half the onion centers and add to meat mixture. Stuff the onions with the mixture and sprinkle remaining cheese on top. Set onions in a buttered baking dish and bake uncovered at 350⁰ for 30 minutes or until cheese is golden.

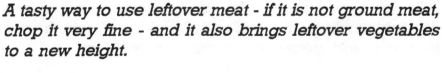

A tasty way to use leftover meat - if it is not ground meat, chop it very fine - and it also brings leftover vegetables to a new height.

POTATO PARMESAN STICKS

1/2 cup grated Parmesan cheese
2 tsp dried oregano
2 8-oz baking potatoes, washed, unpeeled
1 egg white, beaten

Vegetable cooking spray

Combine Parmesan cheese and oregano. Cut each potato lengthwise into 8 wedges; dip into egg white, then coat with cheese mixture. Place potatoes on a baking sheet coated with cooking spray. Bake at 425⁰ for 25 minutes. Four servings.

OVEN FRIED POTATOES

New potatoes, 4 halves per person,
  or 1 russet per person, cut in strips
Garlic cloves, minced
Olive oil

Salt & pepper

Coat potato halves or strips in olive oil. Place in 1 layer in baking dish. Spread minced garlic over cut surfaces and sprinkle with salt and pepper. Bake at 400⁰ for 1 hour.

Putting the potatoes on foil makes them cook faster. You do need to watch them and turn the oven off when they are nicely brown but before they get too dry.

TWICE LIGHT POTATOES

2 large baking potatoes
1/4 cup non-fat cottage cheese
1/4 cup chopped green onions
1 tsp dried dill (or 1 TBS fresh chopped)
Paprika

Salt & pepper

Bake potatoes at 425⁰ for 45 minutes (or microwave for 8 to 10 minutes.) Cut each potato in half lengthwise and scoop out center pulp. If you microwaved, leave a 1/2 inch rim of pulp to support skin. In a small bowl, combine potato centers with cottage cheese, onions, dill, and salt and pepper to taste.

Spoon into potato skins, heaping and mounding. Sprinkle top with paprika. Bake at 350⁰ until hot, about 20 minutes. Serves 4.

Delicious stuffed potatoes with no fat and few calories!

STUFFED POTATOES

2 large baking potatoes
1/4 cup nonfat yogurt
1/4 cup grated Parmesan cheese
1/4 cup minced green onion
2 slices crisp bacon, crumbled

Bake potatoes at 425⁰ for 45 minutes or in microwave for 8 to 10 minutes. Cut each potato in half lengthwise and scoop out centers. If you microwaved leave 1/4 inch pulp to support skins. In a small bowl combine potato pulp with yogurt, onion, bacon, and half the grated cheese. Mix lightly with fork, then pile into shells, heaping and mounding. Sprinkle tops with remaining cheese. Bake at 350⁰ until hot, about 20 minutes. Serves 4.

Use your microwave for crisp, dry BACON. Arrange strips on a stack of 3 paper towels on top of 5 or 6 layers of 1/4 newspaper sheets (so the stack fits in the microwave.) On top of bacon lay 3 more paper towels and layers of newspaper. Cook on HIGH till crisp, about 5 minutes for 5 slices, let stand for an equal period.

POTATOES GRUYERE

2 1/2 lbs new potatoes, peeled
2 1/2 cups shredded Gruyere cheese
1 cup half & half

Salt & pepper

Boil potatoes until almost tender, about 20 minutes.
Drain. Slice THINLY. (The processor slicing is nice.
The potatoes will not get done if not very thin.)
Layer half of potato slices in buttered 2-quart baking
dish. Spread half of cheese over potatoes, salt and
pepper. Layer remaining potatoes. Pour over half-
and-half.
Top with remaining cheese. Bake at 350⁰ for 35
minutes or until golden and potatoes are tender.
Serves 8 or more.

*If you cannot find Gruyere cheese, or it is just too
expensive, Haverti does almost as well.*

*These potatoes were served at a French ski resort with
fresh trout sautéed in butter. Unforgettable!*

POTATOES MEXICAN

6 medium potatoes
4 slices bacon
1 1/2 tsp chili powder
2 TBS chopped fresh parsley (2 tsp dried)

1/2 tsp salt

Boil unpeeled potatoes until tender, let cool and cut into 1/4" slices. Cook bacon till crisp. Remove it to drain, reserving 2 tablespoons bacon grease in skillet. Stir salt and chili powder into bacon drippings. Add potato slices and stir to coat with seasoning.

Place potatoes in a greased 9"x9" baking dish. Sprinkle with bacon bits and parsley. Cover.
(At this point you can let it wait until you are within 1/2 hour of serving.)
Bake at 350° for 25 minutes. Serves 6.

POTATO SALAD

2 medium potatoes, unpeeled
1/2 medium onion, finely chopped
2 ribs celery, chopped
2 TBS sweet pickle relish
1/2 cup Miracle Whip® salad dressing

Salt & pepper

Boil potatoes until tender. Let cool and dice. Combine remaining ingredients, adding more salad dressing if the mixture is too dry. Salt and pepper to taste. Chill. Serves 4.

POTATO SALAD II

As above, except substitute mayonaisse for salad dressing and chopped dill pickles for sweet relish.

POTATO SALAD III TO INFINITY

Everyone's mother made a different potato salad. She may have added chopped hard-cooked eggs or mustard, mashed potatoes instead of diced, included chopped green peppers or pimientos, spiced it with dill or sesame seeds. She may even have used macaroni instead of potatoes.

NEW MEXICAN POTATO SALAD

2 medium potatoes, unpeeled
1/2 cup chopped green onions
1/2 cup chopped jicama
4 oz chopped mild green chile, undrained
1/2 cup mayonaisse

Salt & pepper

Boil potatoes until tender. Let cool and dice. Combine remaining ingredients, adding more mayonaisse if salad is too dry. (If jicama is not available, use celery). Salt and pepper to taste. Chill. Serves 4.

For the New Mexican dish, PAPAS Y CHILES, cook potatoes until starting to fall apart; dice; add onions and chile, salt and pepper. (Omit jicama and mayonaisse.) Serve hot.

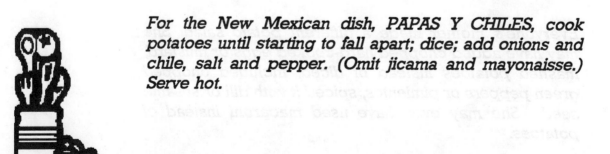

POTATO PANCAKES

2 large potatoes
2 eggs
1/4 cup flour
1/4 cup cream or milk
1/4 cup finely chopped onion

Salt & pepper
4 TBS butter

OPTIONAL: 2 apples, cored & sliced

Peel and finely shred potatoes in the processor or with a grater. Beat eggs with flour, cream and onion. Add potato; salt & pepper to taste.
Over medium heat, melt 2 tablespoons butter in 10-or 12-inch skillet. When hot, add batter by kitchen-spoonfuls (2 tablespoons each), forming ovals. Sauté pancakes on medium heat, 4 minutes each side (8 minutes total). Keep cakes warm in 200^0 oven while you cook the rest of the pancakes.
If desired, sauté apple slices in remaining 2 tablespoons butter until golden.
Serves 4.

Classic with pork, but great with beef and chicken, too.

BUFFET POTATOES

3 1/2 lbs baking potatoes
2 TBS minced fresh dill
    and dill sprigs
1/2 cup butter, melted
1 tsp salt

Peel potatoes and slice very thin, processor slices for example. Put in ice water for a few minutes; drain. Coat bottom and sides of 10" deep-dish pie pan with some of melted butter. Arrange a layer of half the potatoes in the pan, overlapping slices. Sprinkle with 1/2 teaspoon salt and 1 tablespoon minced dill. Spread rest of potatoes. Drizzle with remaining butter and top with remaining salt and minced dill.
Cover the potatoes with waxed paper and then foil. Put another pie pan on top of the foil; weight with a brick.
Bake at 350⁰ for 1 1/2 hours, or until potatoes are tender. Longer baking won't hurt. (Pierce with fork to test.)
Remove weight, pan, foil and paper. Run a knife around edge of potatoes to loosen. Invert onto serving plate and garnish with dill sprigs. Serves 10.

A neat system is to cut the pie into serving slices with a sharp knife before you put it on the buffet, and provide a pie server.

SIMPLE SWEET POTATOES

1 lb sweet potatoes, unpeeled
Garlic salt

Pepper
Vegetable cooking spray

Wash and slice potatoes in 1/4" to 1/2" slices. Layer in shallow baking dish sprayed with vegetable cooking spray. Sprinkle each layer, if you have more than one, with garlic salt and pepper, and spray the top of the slices. Bake, uncovered, at 400⁰ for 30 minutes. Serves 2.

CANDIED SWEET POTATOES

3 medium-size sweet potatoes
1/2 cup light corn syrup
1/2 cup orange juice
1/2 cup chopped pecans

3 TBS butter

Cook sweet potatoes until almost tender - about 10 minutes on HIGH in the microwave, or in boiling water, covered, for about 25 minutes. Peel and slice in 1/4-inch slices. Arrange, slightly overlapping in one layer in buttered shallow baking dish. Mix syrup and orange juice; pour over potatoes. Sprinkle with pecans and dot with butter. Bake at 350⁰ for 30 minutes. Serves 4.

BOURBON YAMS

1 29-oz can whole sweet potatoes, or
    3 medium-size sweet potatoes
1/2 cup brown sugar
1/2 cup orange juice
1/2 cup bourbon
1 tsp cinnamon

6 TBS butter, melted

OPTIONAL: 1/4 cup chopped pecans

Slice canned potatoes in 1/2 inch slices - OR if you are using fresh sweet potatoes, cook until tender, about 10 minutes on HIGH in the microwave; cool, peel and slice. Place slices in a buttered 8"x8" baking dish, overlapping slightly. Combine remaining ingredients except nuts and pour over potatoes. Sprinkle with pecans, if desired.
(At this point you may cover and hold up to 2 hours til ready to heat.)
Bake at 350⁰ for 25 minutes or until thoroughly heated. Serves 4.

This dish tastes as good as if it came right off the old plantation. It adds glamour to a baked ham, or roast chicken or turkey.

RASPBERRY VINEGAR SAUCE

2 egg yolks
1 TBS raspberry vinegar
1/2 tsp sugar
Dash of nutmeg
2 TBS yogurt or sour cream

Salt

In top of double boiler over hot water, whisk together first four ingredients with a dash of salt. When thickened add yogurt or sour cream. Place hot vegetable - beans, carrots, broccoli - in a serving dish and pour the sauce over.

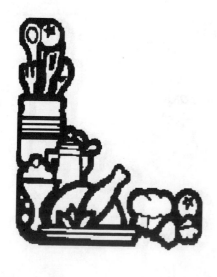

PARSLEY SAUCE

1/4 cup mayonaisse
1/2 cup low-fat yogurt
1/2 cup fresh parsley, finely chopped
1 TBS lemon juice
1 tsp fines herbes

Salt & pepper to taste

Mix and chill. Serve cold with ham or fish mousse, cold vegetables. Also a good salad dressing for a green salad.

When you are having guests, remember cold vegetables. They are cooked ahead and chilled, so you have time to dress them up with a made-ahead sauce. You might julienne carrots, cook until tender, and chill: then serve with this parsley sauce for a tasty, colorful dish.

MUSTARD-DILL SAUCE

1 1/2 tsp dry mustard
1/2 cup Dijon mustard
3 TBS red wine vinegar
1 TBS sugar
1/2 cup chopped fresh dill

1/4 cup oil

Combine all ingredients except oil. Add oil slowly while stirring.

Toss with vegetables - broccoli, green beans, carrots, etc. - or serve over or under fish. Makes 1 cup.

When broccoli has been the only vegetable in the market for months, this will provide a change of flavor.

ASPARAGUS WITH PRIMAVERA SAUCE

2 Italian (small) tomatoes, diced
4 oz fresh mushrooms, diced
1/2 tsp basil
2 tsp fresh lemon juice
1/4 cup yogurt

1 TBS butter
Salt & pepper

(10 to 12 stalks asparagus)

Over medium heat, sauté tomatoes and mushrooms in butter until softened, 3 to 4 minutes. Add basil and lemon juice. Stir in yogurt and heat through. Salt and pepper to taste. Arrange steamed asparagus on platter and top with sauce. Makes about 1 cup sauce, enough for 2 servings.

To steam ASPARAGUS: wash asparagus under running water and snap off large ends. (Snapping instead of cutting eliminates waste, as the stalks break where they are tender.) Place asparagus flat in a large skillet and add an inch or so of water. Cover and bring to boil. Simmer to steam asparagus until tender but not limp, about 15 minutes, depending on the size of the stalks. Drain well before serving.

LAURIE'S CHEESE SAUCE FOR VEGETABLES

3 TBS flour
1 1/2 to 2 cups milk
1/2 lb Velveeta® cheese, diced

3 TBS butter

Melt butter, add flour and cook until bubbly, stirring constantly. Add 1 cup milk; cook and stir until smooth. Stir cheese pieces into hot sauce until melted. Add more milk a little at a time to the consistency you want.
Makes 2 cups.

For a vegetable dish for 2 people, 1/2 the recipe (1 cup) is ample.

You may substitute 1/4 can beer for part of the milk, adding after the cheese to desired consistency.

Use the sauce over any hot vegetable. It is delicious if you add 1/4 cup finely chopped fresh tomatoes.

BREADS

Nothing is more inviting than the smell of bread baking. And nothing tastes better than a loaf or muffin still hot from the oven.

Most recipes in this section are for quick breads that do not require successive periods of rising and kneading. Breads like French, for example, have few ingredients, but the method is more demanding.

If you keep a box of biscuit mix and a packet or two of cornbread mix in your pantry, you can always rescue an otherwise uninspired meal. Remember that the mix makes dumplings and pancakes, too.

Try adding grated cheese or a spice to your biscuits and muffins - dill is excellent in biscuits.

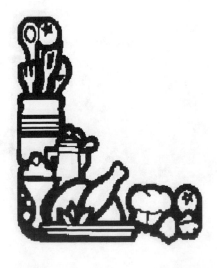

BEER BREAD

4 cups SELF-RISING flour
3/4 cup sugar
1 12-oz bottle beer

Mix flour and sugar. Add beer and mix just until well blended. In a lightly greased and floured loaf pan, bake at 350⁰ for 1 hour, checking after 50 minutes with toothpick test (pick inserted in center should come out clean.)
Allow to cool completely before slicing.

A lovely dense texture, thinly sliced beer bread makes wonderful toast - thickly sliced it is perfect for French toast (dip slices in beaten egg and sauté on both sides in butter.)

DATE MUFFINS

2 cups biscuit mix
2 TBS sugar
1 egg
1 cup date pieces

Mix biscuit mix, sugar, and egg with 2/3 cup water. Beat until well blended. Stir in dates. Fill bottom-greased muffin cups about 2/3 full. Bake at 400⁰ about 15 minutes or until golden. Makes 12 muffins.

You may add a cup of raisins, nuts, or chopped apple, instead of the dates or a combination of fruit and nuts.

CRUNCHY BISCUITS

3 oz cheddar cheese, grated
1 cup SELF-RISING flour
1 cup crushed corn flakes
1 egg, beaten
1 TBS milk

1/2 cup butter, softened
Salt & pepper

Cream butter with cheese, a pinch each of salt and pepper, flour and cornflakes. Combine egg and milk. Reserving 2 teaspoons for glazing, add egg and milk to flour mixture. Blend thoroughly. Roll teaspoonfuls of dough into balls and place 2 inches apart on lightly greased cookie sheet. Flatten tops with fork and glaze with reserved egg mixture. Bake at 350^0 for 10 to 12 minutes. Cool on cookie sheet; transfer to rack to crisp. Makes about 3 dozen.

FLAKY BREAD STICKS

1 lb pkg frozen filo pastry, thawed
1/2 cup (1 stick) butter, melted

OPTIONAL: garlic salt

Unroll 2 or 3 inches of filo pastry, keeping a towel on unrolled portion so it will not dry out. With a very sharp knife, cut a 1/2 inch strip through all layers of dough. Brush top and cut edge with melted butter. Using one third of 1/2 inch wide stack of pastry, twist gently to form a long spiral. Place on buttered cookie sheet.
Brush top of remaining stack with butter and, using half of remaining stack, make another curling breadstick. Brush top of last third and repeat.
Cut another 1/2 inch strip, etc. Repeat process with all the filo pastry. Sprinkle with garlic salt, if desired. Bake at 400⁰ for 8 to 10 minutes or until golden.
Makes about 4 dozen.

Time consuming but well worth the trouble, these light sticks seem to melt in your mouth. Filo may be difficult to work with at first, but by the time you finish the pound you will be twisting dough like an expert.

SAUSAGE BISCUITS

1/2 lb Jimmy Dean® pork sausage
1 cup biscuit mix

Mix sausage, biscuit mix, and 1/3 cup water. Drop by tablespoonfuls on cookie sheet. Bake at 450⁰ until golden brown, 20 to 30 minutes. Makes 8 to 12 biscuits.

These are so good you may want to double the recipe if there are more than 2 or 3 diners.

Drop by teaspoonfuls for smaller biscuits and you have very popular appetizers. The smaller size bake for 15 to 20 minutes. Be sure to use a lean sausage.

CORN BISCUIT FINGERS

9-oz can cream corn
2 cups biscuit mix

1/2 stick butter

Melt butter in shallow baking pan.

Combine corn and biscuit mix. Roll or pat into 6" x 10" rectangle. Cut into 1" x 3" fingers. Place biscuits in buttered pan, turning to coat both sides.
Bake at 450⁰ until golden, 10 to 12 minutes.

These are delicious tidbits to use as hors d'oeuvres as well as with a meal.

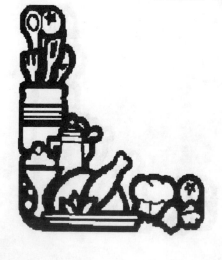

CHEESE BISCUITS

2 cups biscuit mix
1/3 to 1/2 cup beer
1/4 cup finely chopped green onion
1/2 cup grated cheddar cheese.

Combine biscuit mix, onions and cheese. Add beer gradually. Stir with a fork to form a sticky ball. Turn onto a lightly floured board, and knead 8 to 10 times; roll or pat to 1/2 inch thick. Cut with a biscuit cutter, or the floured edge of a juice glass. Bake on a lightly greased cookie sheet at 450⁰ for 10 to 12 minutes until golden. Yield; 16 biscuits.

For a variation, you may substitute 1/4 cup chopped fresh dill for the onions.

TEXAS CORNBREAD

1 6 1/2-oz pkg yellow cornbread mix
3 TBS chili powder

Add chili powder to dry mix. Make cornbread according to package directions.
Makes 6 muffins or 9 sticks.

Three tablespoons of chili powder makes the cornbread noticeably hot. You may want to adjust for your taste.

There is no question that fresh bread lifts any meal out of the ordinary.

SESAME EGG ROLLS

3 to 3 1/2 cups flour
2 TBS sugar
2 envelopes fast-rising dry yeast
2 eggs
2 tsp sesame seeds

2 TBS oil
1 1/2 tsp salt

In a large bowl, combine 3 cups flour, sugar, yeast, and salt; mix thoroughly. Separate 1 egg; reserve white. Mix yolk, remaining egg, and oil, with 1 cup hot water. Add to dry ingredients. Mix until smooth with a wooden spoon, stirring vigorously. Turn out on floured surface. Knead until smooth and elastic, 8 or 10 times. If the dough is sticky, add flour. Cover and let sit 5 minutes.
Divide and shape dough into 16 balls and arrange in greased 9-inch round cake pan. Brush rolls with beaten reserved egg white. Sprinkle with sesame seeds.
Cover with a towel and let rise until doubled in bulk. (Dough will rise in about 25 minutes if you set pan on a rack in a baking dish and add boiling water to just under rack.)
Bake at 350⁰ about 20 minutes, or until rolls are golden and sound hollow when tapped on the bottom. Makes 16 rolls.

SPOONBREAD

2 cups evaporated skimmed milk
1 cup cornmeal
2 eggs, separated

2 TBS butter
1/2 tsp salt
Vegetable cooking spray

Combine milk, cornmeal, butter, and salt with 1 cup water. Stir and cook over medium heat until thickened, about 5 minutes. Remove from heat.
In electric mixer, beat egg whites until stiff; at slower speed, add yolks. Gradually stir about 1/3 of hot mixture into eggs; while stirring, add eggs to remaining hot mixture.
In a 1-quart baking dish coated with cooking spray, bake at 350° for 35 minutes, or until knife inserted in center comes out clean. Serves 8-9.

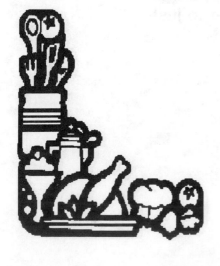

YOGURT BISCUITS

1 cup SELF-RISING flour
1/2 cup (1 stick) margarine, softened
1/2 cup yogurt (or sour cream)

Combine ingredients. Drop by spoonfuls on buttered cookie sheet. Bake at 350⁰ until golden, about 15 to 20 minutes.
Teaspoonfuls will make 2 dozen crusty little biscuits; tablespoonfuls 1 dozen larger ones.

These freeze well if put in an airtight plastic bag.

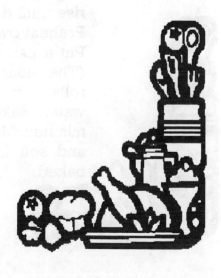

BOLILLOS
(MEXICAN ROLLS)

1 1/2 pkgs (1 1/2 TBS) active dry yeast
3/4 cup warm water
2 1/4 cups flour
1/2 tsp salt
FOR GLAZE: 1 egg white with 1 TBS water

Sprinkle the yeast on the water and let stand till dissolved, about 5 minutes. Stir in salt. Pour in processor bowl (with metal chopping blade.) Add 1 cup flour, process 4 seconds. Add another cup of flour, process 5 seconds. Add remaining 1/4 cup flour, process 10 seconds. If dough is too sticky, add up to another 1/4 cup flour. Process 1 minute. Dough will form ball at top of spindle. Place dough in oiled mixing bowl, turning ball of dough to grease all around. Cover with a dry cloth and let rise in a warm place until doubled in size, about 1 1/2 or 2 hours.

Punch the dough down. On lightly floured board, knead for 2 or 3 minutes. Form into long roll about 2" in diameter. Divide into pieces 2" to 3" long and put on ungreased baking sheet. Cover with towel and allow to rise until double in size, about 1 hour.

Preheat oven to 450⁰.

Put a pan of hot water on floor or bottom shelf of oven. (The steam is necessary for the bread texture.) Brush rolls with the egg white beaten with 1 tablespoon cold water. Bake at 450⁰ until golden brown, about 20 to 30 minutes. Makes about 8 bolillos. These are crusty outside, and soft inside, and must be eaten the day they are baked.

SALADS

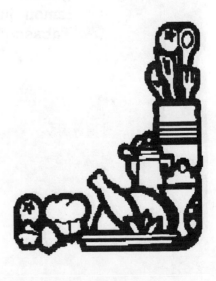

The first rule for salads is to use the freshest things available. You cannot always decide on your salad before you go to the market - wait to see what looks crisp and full of flavor.

Salads may be tossed, arranged, or molded. Each type has its own advantages.

The basic tossed salad is the quickest. Cut or tear greens into bite-size pieces; toss them together or with other cut up vegetables; shake up vinegar, oil, and seasoning for a dressing.

A salad arranged on a large platter looks elegant on a buffet, and individual arranged plates decorate a dinner table. You can even complement your decor with the ingredients - red peppers, purple onions, orange carrots, and greens, of course.

The great advantage of a molded salad is that it can be, must be, made ahead. Almost any finely chopped fresh ingredients lend themselves to being combined with plain gelatin for large or individual molds. Remember to use lemon juice, salt and pepper, horseradish sauce, or Tabasco® to keep it from being too bland.

SALSA ASPIC SALAD

1 3-oz package lemon Jello®
1 cup mild fresh salsa or chili sauce or
    picante sauce

1 cup boiling water

Dissolve Jello® in boiling water. Add salsa. Chill,
unmold, serve.

Good with a dressing of avocado mashed with salt,
pepper, and lemon juice. Serves 4.

*This is one of those incredibly good recipes that is so
easy you may want to keep it a secret.*

ITALIAN FLAG SALAD

1 head romaine lettuce
1/2 lb mozzarella cheese
2 red bell peppers
2 TBS chopped fresh basil

1/2 cup vinaigrette; or oil, vinegar, salt, and
    pepper whisked together

Arrange lettuce leaves around outside edge of a
large plate. Seed and cut red peppers into 1-inch
wide strips, place in circle on lettuce. Cut cheese in
3" x 1" slices, place in smaller circle on top of
peppers, ends meeting in the middle of the plate.
Drizzle with vinaigrette or oil and vinegar. Sprinkle
with basil. Serves 6.

*Named for the colors it shares with the Italian flag, this is
a handsome buffet salad.*

AMBROSIA SALAD

1 cup coconut
1 cup Mandarin orange slices
1 cup chunk pineapple, drained
1 cup miniature marshmallows
1 cup sour cream (or yogurt)

Combine all ingredients. Cover and chill overnight.
Serves 8.

This is sweet and pretty enough for dessert - just
serve it in sherbet glasses.

*Ambrosia is a traditional treat for family holiday dinners.
Children love it, and it complements a roast turkey nicely.*

COLE SLAW

1 head cabbage, finely chopped
2 small onions, finely chopped
1/2 bottle cole slaw dressing

Combine and chill before serving.
The secret to good slaw is a fine texture. The grater
on the processor does a good job. Serves 6-8.

There are MYRIAD VARIATIONS on the basic idea.
To the above, add one or more of the following:

1/2 cup raisins
1 apple, unpeeled, cored, chopped
1 or 2 carrots, grated
1/4 cup finely chopped pickles (or pickle relish)
1 red or green bell pepper, finely chopped

*Cole slaw is practically required for picnics and bar-b-
ques.*

SUNSET SALAD

1 15-oz can sliced beets
6 oranges
1/4 cup chopped green onion
1/2 cup walnut or pecan halves
1/2 tsp ground ginger

1/4 cup salad oil
Salt & pepper

Peel oranges and cut into segments, saving 1/4 cup orange juice for dressing. Pile orange segments in a 6" diameter circle in the middle of a serving plate.
Cut beet slices into 1/8" strips; arrange in a circle around outside of oranges, strips extending ray-like from oranges toward outside of plate.
Sprinkle onions and nuts over.

For dressing, in a screw-top jar combine reserved orange juice with ginger, salad oil, and salt and pepper to taste. Shake to mix well; spoon over salad.

SPINACH SALAD

1 bunch fresh spinach
2 slices bacon
1/4 cup finely chopped green onion
3 TBS red wine vinegar
1 hard-cooked egg, grated

Salt & pepper

Wash, remove stems, and coarsely chop spinach. Fry bacon till crisp. Drain, reserving 1 TBS bacon grease. Crumble bacon. Combine bacon grease, onion, vinegar and bacon bits, salt and pepper to taste. Shake or stir to mix well. Toss with spinach. Sprinkle grated egg over top.

For a heartier salad, add diced cheese or seasoned croutons; or sprinkle grated cheese on top.

JULY FOURTH SALAD

4 medium tomatoes, sliced thinly
1 medium onion, sliced thinly
1 cucumber, sliced thinly
1/2 cup vinegar
1 TBS sugar

Salt & pepper to taste

Arrange tomatoes, onion and cucumber in shallow dish. Pour vinegar over - it should barely cover slices - and sprinkle with sugar, salt and pepper. Chill for at least 1 hour, turning occasionally. Serves 4-6.

Perfect for the holiday it is named for, this salad travels to picnics in great shape. When you make it ahead, put it in a snap-cover plastic dish to chill. It is ready to go.

RUSSIAN SALAD

Salad greens for 4 to 6
1 2-oz can anchovy fillets, undrained
1/4 cup vinegar
3 TBS chili sauce

1/4 cup salad oil
1/8 tsp pepper

Break greens into bite-size pieces. Cut fillets into 3
or 4 pieces each; combine them, their oil, salad oil,
vinegar, chili sauce and pepper. Pour over greens
and toss lightly.
Serves 4 to 6.

*Salads have a crisper texture if greens do not soak in the
dressing, though a dressing usually improves if made
ahead and allowed to chill. Add dressing and toss just
before serving.*

FRUIT SALAD BRENDA
Dessert or Salad

1 banana, peeled & sliced
1 apple, unpeeled, cored & chopped
1 small can chunk pineapple, drained
1 pt strawberries, washed & sliced
4 oz yogurt, vanilla or fruit flavored

Combine gently (don't batter fruit) and allow to chill for at least an hour. Do not make it the day before, however. Serves 6.

Use your imagination and what you have in the refrigerator to create your own version. Pecans or walnuts are very good, along with any fruit. Mangos and kiwis give an exotic flavor.

MANGO & TOMATO SALAD

1 large ripe mango
4 plum tomatoes
1 tsp white wine vinegar
5 large fresh basil leaves
1/8 tsp curry powder

1 1/2 TBS olive oil
Salt & pepper

Pit and peel mango, and cut in 1/2" slices.
Cut tomatoes into 1/2" wedges. Arrange alternate slices of mango and tomato on 4 individual or 1 large plate.
In processor, combine oil with basil, curry powder, salt & pepper (or mince basil with sharp knife and whisk ingredients together.)
When ready to serve, spoon dressing over mango and tomatoes. Serves 4.

BLUE CHEESE DRESSING

2 oz blue cheese
1/2 cup ricotta cheese
2 TBS sherry
2 TBS wine vinegar
2 tsp garlic salt

Crumble blue cheese. Combine all ingredients. Cover; refrigerate at least 1 hour, 4 would be better or overnight. Makes about 1 cup.

This is a strong flavored dressing, so use it sparingly at first.

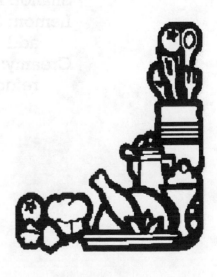

VINAIGRETTE DRESSING

BASIC

1/2 cup olive oil
1/4 cup red or white wine vinegar
1/2 tsp Dijon-style mustard
Dash of black pepper

Stir well before spooning small amount over salad.
Makes 3/4 cup. It will keep in a closed jar in the
refrigerator for up to a week.

VARIATIONS

Add to basic recipe,

Garlic: Add 1 clove garlic, mashed.
Herb: Add a pinch of basil, oregano, or fines
     herbs.
Tomato: Add 2 tablespoons tomato juice.
Shallot: Add 1 teaspoon finely minced shallots.
Lemon: Substitute lemon juice for vinegar and
     add a dash of grated lemon rind.
Creamy: Add 1/2 cup non-fat yogurt. Keep
     refrigerated.

DESSERTS

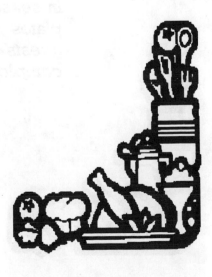

Desserts are the best-loved part of a meal for many people, and it is easy to make many delicious types.

Cookies are especially versatile because they may be served with coffee, a custard, fruit, or ice cream, besides being enjoyed for snacks.

There are so many good cake mixes available that we have included only a few recipes for those times you can't get to the store or are just in the mood to bake. The icing is the secret of most cakes.

Canned pie fillings, especially fruit fillings, are also numerous and tasty, and easy to make. We felt the pies included here were worth special attention.

Frozen desserts should be high on your list, not only for their convenience of being made ahead, but because the cool sweetness complements any meal.

Finally, consider building a lovely fruit centerpiece with bananas, apples, plums, peaches - whatever is in season. When you serve the coffee, pass dessert plates and fruit (or steak) knives, and invite your guests to help themselves. A choice of cheeses completes a perfect ending.

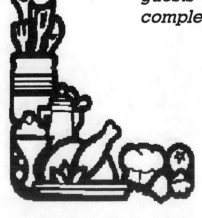

AMARETTI

1 8-oz can (or pkg) almond paste
1 cup sugar
2 egg whites
1 can chocolate fudge icing

NOTE: If you have **MARZIPAN** instead of almond paste, omit sugar.

Dice almond paste. Combine with sugar and egg whites and mix until smooth. Drop teaspoonfuls onto paper-lined cookie sheets. (Use grocery bag brown paper cut to fit pan.) Bake at 325^0 for 25 to 30 minutes. Cool. These are difficult to remove unless you wet the back of the paper. To do this, put a little water to cover the bottom of the cookie sheet and lay the paper with the cookies on it. After a few minutes the cookies will lift off.
Stick the flat sides of two cookies together with icing and let dry. Store in air tight container.
Makes about 2 dozen.

DUMP CAKE HELEN

1 can blueberry pie filling
1 box lemon cake mix
1 16-oz can crushed pineapple, undrained
1/4 cup chopped pecans
1/4 cup grated coconut

1 stick butter

Dump pie filling into 9"x13" pan and spread. Spread pineapple on top of filling. Sprinkle cake mix on pineapple. Dot with butter. Sprinkle coconut and nuts over top. Bake at 350°; 1/2 hour uncovered, then cover with foil and bake 40 minutes more; a total of 1 hour, 10 minutes. Serves 20-24.

Also try it with apple pie filling and spice cake mix, or cherry and chocolate - a good dessert to take to a gathering.

PRALINE KISSES

1 cup light brown sugar
1 egg white
1 1/2 cups pecan halves or pieces

In small bowl of electric mixer, beat egg white until it forms stiff peaks. Add brown sugar gradually, beating constantly. Fold in nuts by hand. Drop by teaspoonfuls onto greased cookie sheet. Bake at 250⁰ for 30 minutes. Remove from pan immediately and cool. Makes 3 dozen.

An attractive variation on a plate of cookies, and a cannot-stop-at-one morsel.

SAND TARTS

1/4 cup confectioner's sugar
1 cup flour
1/2 cup chopped pecans
1/2 tsp vanilla

1/4 lb butter, softened

Cream softened butter and sugar together. Add flour, nuts, vanilla, and stir well. Using 1 rounded teaspoon dough each, shape into balls or traditional crescents. (For crescent, form into 3" x 1/2" roll and curve.) Bake on ungreased cookie sheet at 325⁰ for 20 minutes or until light brown. Dust with powdered sugar while warm. Makes 2 1/2 dozen.

The doubled recipe is also simple and successful.

A favorite cookie of the South, this one tastes just as it should.

VANILLA FINGERS

1/3 cup sugar
1 egg, well beaten
1 teaspoon vanilla
3/4 cup flour
1/4 cup finely chopped pecans

1/2 cup butter, softened

In an electric mixer, cream butter and sugar together.
Add egg, flour, and vanilla. In a shallow, buttered 8"
x 8" pan, spread batter with a knife first dipped in
cold water. Sprinkle with nuts. Bake at 375^0 about 10
to 15 minutes, until lightly browned.
Cut into fingers while still warm. Makes 2 dozen.

When cool, store in airtight container.

*A nice cookie for a tea party, the recipe can be doubled
and baked in a 9" x 13" pan.*

OATMEAL CRUMBLES

1 cup brown sugar
1 tsp vanilla
2 cups quick oatmeal

1/2 cup butter, softened

Combine ingredients in order given. Spread evenly into well buttered 8" x 8" pan. Bake at 350⁰ for 20 to 25 minutes. Let cool 5 minutes before cutting into squares.

Remove squares from pan while slightly warm. (If they cool completely you will have to pry them out with a fork.)
Makes 9 squares or 12 fingers.

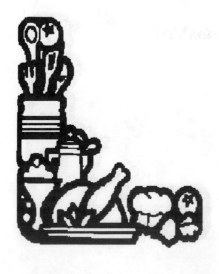

COCONUT DROPS

3/4 cup sweetened condensed milk
8 oz shredded coconut
2 tsp vanilla
1 cup slivered almonds

Mix all ingredients. Drop by teaspoonfuls onto a well buttered cookie sheet. Bake at 300⁰ for 10 minutes. Makes 4 dozen.

Coconut is a food you can tint to match your table decor, if you wish. For example, if you fancy a pink cookie, add red food coloring to the coconut before you mix the batter.

PUMPKIN COOKIES

1/2 cup sugar
2 eggs
1 cup canned pumpkin pie mix
2 cups biscuit mix

1/4 cup (1/2 stick) butter, softened

Beat softened butter and sugar at medium speed of an electric mixer until light and fluffy. Add eggs. At lower speed add pumpkin, and then biscuit mix. Drop by teaspoonfuls on greased cookie sheet. Sprinkle tops with sugar. Bake at 350° for 15 minutes. Makes 4 dozen.

For Thanksgiving or Halloween, push a candy corn kernel into top of each cookie after baking.

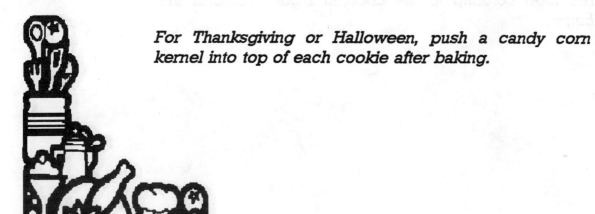

RUM BALLS

1 17-oz pkg vanilla wafers
2 cups nuts (walnuts, pecans, or almonds)
2 TBS cocoa
1/2 cup light corn syrup
1/4 cup dark rum

OPTIONAL: confectioner's sugar

In processor (or blender) grind vanilla wafers and nuts very fine. Mix with cocoa, syrup and rum. Using rounded teaspoonfuls, form into balls. (This is easier if you dust your hands with powdered sugar.) Let dry for about an hour, then roll in sugar, if desired. Store in an air-tight container. They are better after several days. Makes 30.

If you use bourbon instead of rum, you have WHISKEY BALLS. Indispensible for a holiday cookie assortment, rum or whiskey balls make welcome gifts.

LAURA'S COOKIES

1 cup sugar
1 egg
1 cup chunky peanut butter

Combine ingredients. Drop by teaspoonfuls on lightly greased cookie sheet. Flatten cookies with a fork dipped in sugar. Bake at 350⁰ for 10 minutes. When partially cool remove to rack to crisp. Store in airtight container. Makes about 3 dozen.

If there is a beginning cook at your house, suggest these.

SCOTTISH SHORTBREAD

1 cup butter
2 cups flour
1/2 cup confectioner's sugar

Sift the dry ingredients into the processor bowl. Add cold butter cut in large pieces. Process until the stiff dough forms.
(Without a processor, allow butter to soften and blend dry ingredients into it.)
Pat into an ungreased 9" x 9" inch pan. Press edges down. Cut into fingers or squares, and pierce through dough with fork every 1/2 inch. Bake at 325⁰ for 35 to 40 minutes. Recut and let cool 10 minutes before removing to rack. Makes about 2 dozen fingers.

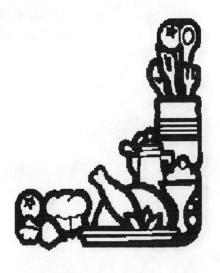

ALMOND COOKIES

1/4 cup sugar
1 egg yolk
1 teaspoon almond extract
1 1/4 cups all-purpose flour

1/2 cup butter, softened
1 tablespoon water

Beat softened butter and sugar at medium speed of an electric mixer until light and fluffy. Add egg yolk, water, and almond extract. Beat well. Stir in flour.

This is a stiff dough suitable for a cookie press. Otherwise, make small balls from a teaspoon of dough, place on ungreased cookie sheet and flatten with a fork. Bake at 400⁰ for 6 minutes or until lightly browned. Remove from cookie sheet and cool completely on wire racks. Store in air tight container. Makes about 3 dozen.

TARA WHITE ICING

2 1/4 cups sugar
3 TBS light corn syrup
3 egg whites, beaten stiff
2 TBS confectioners' sugar

1/2 cup water

Cook sugar, water, and corn syrup to soft ball stage, 238⁰ on a candy thermometer. While beating, slowly add hot mixture to stiff but not dry egg whites. Beat until icing is smooth and creamy and beat in confectioners' sugar. This makes enough icing to fill and ice a layer cake, or ice two loaf cakes.

You may add coconut, lemon juice, crushed strawberries, or whatever your imagination suggests.

QUICK BUTTER ICING

2 1/2 cups confectioner's sugar
3 to 4 TBS milk
1 tsp vanilla

1/2 cup butter, softened
1/4 tsp salt

Cream softened butter and sugar at medium speed of an electric mixer until light and fluffy. Add salt, flavoring, and milk as needed. If you use one of the liquid flavorings suggested below, adjust the amount of milk accordingly.

Some flavor options are as follows:
1 tsp almond extract OR
2 TBS rum or liqueur OR
2 TBS instant coffee OR
Juice and grated zest of 1 lemon OR
Juice and grated zest of 1 orange OR
2 squares of bitter chocolate, melted.

Consider using two flavors in a cake - lemon for filling and vanilla for icing, or coffee and chocolate. Just divide your icing in half and flavor each separately.

SPONGE LAYER CAKE

3/4 cup sugar
4 eggs, room temperature
1/2 teaspoon almond extract
3/4 cups flour
1 tsp baking powder

1/4 tsp salt
2 TBS water

Combine and sift flour, baking powder and salt.
Separate eggs. In the small bowl of your electric mixer, beat the whites until stiff. While beating, slowly add half of the sugar. In the large bowl of mixer, beat egg yolks until thick and gradually add remaining sugar. Continue beating as you add almond flavoring and water. Fold in egg whites by hand, one third at a time.
Line an 8" x 16" jelly roll pan with waxed paper and spread in dough. Bake at 375⁰ for 15 to 18 minutes. Invert on rack and remove paper. When cool, cut in half and stack; fill and ice as desired. Makes an 8" x 8" layer cake.

POUND CAKE

2 cups sugar
6 eggs, room temperature
1 1/2 tsp nutmeg
2 cups sifted flour

1 cup butter, softened
1/2 tsp salt

In an electric mixer, beat softened butter with nutmeg and salt. Add sugar gradually and beat at medium speed until light and fluffy. Add eggs, one at a time, blending well. Beat in flour gradually.
Pour the batter into an ungreased, removable rim tube cake pan. Bake at 350⁰ for 1 hour.
Invert and let the cake hang for 1 or 2 hours until it is set.

You may substitute lemon juice for the nutmeg if you prefer.

For a LITTLE CAKE, use half the ingredients and bake in a 4"x8" loaf pan, the bottom lined with waxed paper. It still needs an hour's baking.

Pound cake is endlessly variable. Try it with rum or lemon sauce, ice cream, or any pureed fruit.

PAT-IN PIE CRUST

1 1/2 cups flour
2 TBS sugar
2 TBS milk
1/2 tsp salt
1/2 cup Wesson® oil

Mix dry ingredients. Add oil, milk and mix. Put it in a pie pan and pat it out. Use as unbaked shell or bake at 300⁰ for 25 to 30 minutes.

The dough is too short to make a lattice crust, but you can cut shapes with a cookie cutter to place on top of a fruit pie. Brush the top of the pastry with a little milk for a nice browning, or sprinkle it with sugar.

MERINGUE FOR PIE

2 or 3 egg whites, room temperature
3 TBS sugar
1/4 tsp cream of tartar (optional)

In small bowl of electric mixer, beat egg whites until foamy. Add sugar gradually, and cream of tartar, while continuing beating. Continue beating at high speed of mixer until stiff peaks form. Spread some meringue around edge of pie filling, being sure it touches crust all around so it will not shrink, then fill in center. Bake at 350⁰ until peaks are golden, about 10 to 15 minutes.

PECAN PIE

1 cup sugar
1 cup light corn syrup
4 eggs, beaten
1 tsp vanilla
1 cup pecan halves

1/4 tsp salt
1/3 cup butter
1 unbaked 9-inch pie shell

Stir sugar, syrup and butter over low heat until butter is melted and sugar dissolved. Cool slightly. Add eggs, vanilla, and salt. Mix thoroughly. Pour into pie shell. Arrange pecan halves in concentric circles on top. Bake at 325^0 for 50 minutes to 1 hour.

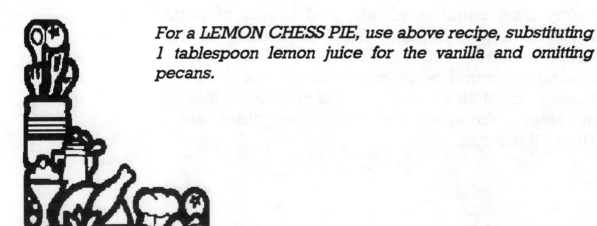

For a LEMON CHESS PIE, use above recipe, substituting 1 tablespoon lemon juice for the vanilla and omitting pecans.

CRUMB PIE CRUST

1/4 to 1/2 cup sugar
1/3 cup butter, melted
1 1/4 cups crumbs

For crumbs, use graham crackers,
zwieback, gingersnaps, vanilla or
chocolate wafers, finely crushed

Crush any of the above in processor or by putting in a plastic bag and rolling with a rolling pin or bottle.

Combine ingredients. Reserve 3 tablespoons of mixture. Press crumbs into bottom and sides of pie plate, using your fingers or a large spoon, and finish by pressing a pie plate of the same size into crust. You may cook the crust in the oven at 350⁰ for 10 minutes OR microwave on HIGH for 1 1/2 to 3 minutes OR chill in the refrigerator for 30 minutes. If cooked, allow to cool before filling.
Fill pie and sprinkle reserved crumbs on top.

The flavor of the filling determines the choice of crumbs.
You may vary the crust with the addition of 1/2 cup finely
chopped nuts, or 1/4 cup grated cheese, or 1/2 teaspoon
cinnamon, or 2 tablespoons cocoa.

CREAM PIE

1/2 cup sugar
2 TBS cornstarch
2 1/2 cups milk
4 egg yolks, beaten
2 tsp vanilla

1/2 tsp salt
Baked pie shell or crumb crust

In 1 1/2-qt casserole mix sugar, salt, and cornstarch. Gradually stir in milk. Microwave on HIGH for 7 minutes, stirring every 3 minutes until slightly thickened. Stir half the thickened mixture into beaten egg yolks. Return mixture to casserole, blending well. Microwave at MEDIUM 4 to 5 minutes more, stirring after 2 minutes. Cool, then stir in vanilla. Allow to cool slightly before pouring into crust.

Use the egg whites to make a meringue for the pie, or Praline Kisses or Amaretti.Use this recipe for custard sauce for a fruit parfait, or to combine with cake. If the double boiler has frustrated you, this is the answer!

For CHOCOLATE CREAM PIE, increase sugar to 1 cup and melt 2 oz unsweetened chocolate with the hot milk mixture; for BANANA CREAM PIE, peel and thinly slice 2 bananas and layer slices in the crust before you pour in cream filling; for COCONUT CREAM PIE, add 1 cup grated coconut to hot mixture, and sprinkle filling with 1/4 cup coconut.

LEMON CUSTARD PIE

1 cup sugar
4 eggs, well beaten
1 lemon, juiced and zest grated
2 tsp flour
1 cup light corn syrup

4 tsp butter, softened
Unbaked 9" pie shell

Mix sugar and flour; add to beaten eggs. Beat in softened butter, syrup, lemon rind and juice.
Pour into uncooked pie crust; bake at 350⁰ for 1 hour, or until table knife inserted in center comes out clean. Do not refrigerate.

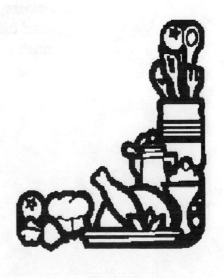

APPLE PIE

1/2 cup sugar
1/2 tsp cinnamon
6 cups apples, peeled & sliced
1/2 cup flour
3/4 cup brown sugar

1/3 cup butter
Unbaked 9" pie shell

Toss together sugar, cinnamon, apples, and 1 TBS of the flour. Arrange in pie shell. Mix butter, brown sugar and remaining flour, by hand or in processor until mixture resembles coarse meal. Sprinkle over apples. Bake at 425⁰ for 30 to 45 minutes, or until apples are tender.

To the topping, you can add 1 cup of crushed cheese crackers - or you can sprinkle individual pie servings with grated cheese and run them under the broiler very briefly to melt the cheese.

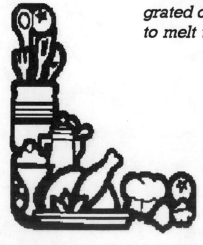

APPLE ALMOND CRISP

1 21-oz can apple pie filling
1 tsp cinnamon
1/2 cup brown sugar
1/2 cup sliced almonds
1 cup flour

7 TBS butter, finely diced
1/8 tsp salt

Pour apple pie filling into buttered 1 1/2 quart baking dish. Sprinkle cinnamon over filling. Mix with fingers until crumbly: flour, sugar, salt and 6 TBS butter. Combine 1/4 cup almonds with flour mixture. Sprinkle evenly over apples. Dot with remaining butter and spread remaining almonds. Bake, uncovered, at 375° for 40 to 45 minutes, or until beginning to brown. Serves 4 to 6.

Serve the crisp on a dessert plate accompanied by a wedge of cheddar; or in a dessert bowl and pass a pitcher of cream or whipped cream.

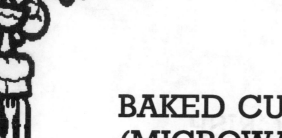

BAKED CUSTARD
(MICROWAVE)

1/4 cup sugar
3 eggs
1/2 tsp vanilla
1 1/3 cups milk
Dash of nutmeg

1/4 tsp salt

Microwave milk in 2-cup measure at HIGH for 2 to 3 1/2 minutes, or until edges bubble. Combine eggs, sugar, salt and vanilla in large bowl. Blend in milk with whisk. Pour into 4 6-oz custard cups and sprinkle with nutmeg.
Arrange cups in a circle around outer edge of oven. Microwave at MEDIUM-HIGH (70%) until custard is soft set, 4 to 7 minutes, turning cups after half the time if your oven does not have a carousel. The center firms as the custard cools. Chill at least 2 hours before serving. Serves 4.

Experiment with your microwave to find the exact cooking time that produces a firm but not dry custard.

FLAN CASA FUENTE

4 eggs
1 14-oz can sweetened condensed milk
1/2 tsp canela (cinnamon)
1/2 tsp grated lemon zest

Beat eggs well. Add milk, 1 cup water, canela and lemon peel. Mix well. Pour into buttered mold, or custard cups. Place in larger pan containing hot water to level of custard. Bake at 350° for 1 hour or until knife inserted in center comes out clean. Cool completely.
Loosen custard with knife; invert on serving platter or individual plates. Serves 6.

Various toppings may be used: maple syrup, caramel, jams, etc.

CARAMEL GLAZE

1 cup sugar
2 TBS water

Combine sugar and water in a heavy skillet. Cook, stirring constantly until caramelized and syrupy. Immediately pour into warm buttered cups or mold. Tilt to coat bottom and sides while sugar is hot. Add custard mixture, cook as above.

GEORGIA PEACH COBBLER

3/4 cup biscuit mix
3/4 cup sugar
3/4 cup milk
1/4 tsp almond extract
1 16-oz pkg frozen sliced peaches, thawed
and drained, or 2 cups fresh, sliced

1/4 cup butter, melted

Cover bottom of an 8"x8" baking dish with melted butter. Combine biscuit mix, sugar, milk, and almond extract. Pour mixture into dish, over butter, without stirring. Layer peaches on top. Bake at 350⁰ for about 1 hour, or until golden.

If you leave peach cobbler on the kitchen table when the children come home from school, don't count on it for supper!

ICE CREAM & CAKE SANDY

2 half gallons ice cream (2 flavors), softened
1 angel food cake, cut in 1-inch cubes

1/2 cup sugar
1/2 cup rum
1 tsp butter

Spread one half-gallon of softened ice cream in 9"x12" pan. Add layer of angel food cake cubes. Top with second half gallon of softened ice cream. Freeze. Serve with rum glaze (or a hot fudge sauce.) Serves 20-24.

Rum Glaze: Microwave sugar, rum, butter with 1/4 cup water on HIGH for 2 minutes. Stir. Microwave on HIGH for 1 1/2 minutes. Stir. Cool to warm before serving.

Pairs of ice cream flavors might be, for example: cherry almond & pistachio almond; chocolate & vanilla; strawberry & chocolate.

A birthday party winner! Ice cream is always a crowd pleaser, and the cake is already in it.

STRAWBERRY ICE CREAM PIE

1 graham cracker crumb pie crust
1 quart strawberry ice cream, softened
1 pint fresh strawberries
4 oz frozen whipped topping, thawed

Fill pie crust with ice cream. Cover with whipped topping and freeze. To serve, decorate with washed and hulled fresh strawberries.
A 9-inch pie serves 6 or 8.

Peach or blueberry would be good, too.

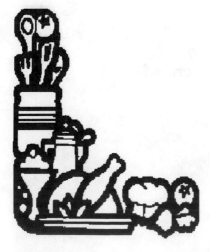

RASPBERRY BRANDY SHERBET

1 8-oz carton plain low-fat yogurt
1/2 cup orange juice
1/3 cup honey
2 cups frozen raspberries, partially thawed

OPTIONAL: 1/4 cup brandy

Combine all ingredients in processor and process until raspberries are finely chopped. Pour into 8-inch square pan and freeze until almost firm. Break into pieces into processor and process until fluffy but not thawed. Return mixture to pan. Sherbet will not be hard frozen. (If you do not use brandy, it will freeze hard, so let stand at room temperature for 10 minutes before serving. Makes 9 servings.

Why not make a recipe of Amaretti to go with the sherbet? Both are simple, made ahead, and it is an elegant dessert.

LEMON-GINGER SHERBET

1 cup sugar
1/4 tsp ground ginger
2 lemons
1/4 cup minced crystallized ginger
1/2 cup brandy

2 cups water

Combine water, sugar, and ground ginger, and bring to a boil, stirring constantly. Allow to cool. Grate zest (thin yellow rind) of 1 lemon to make 1 1/2 tablespoons. Juice both lemons; add water to lemon juice to make 1 cup. Combine lemon zest and juice with sugar mixture. Freeze in ice tray or shallow pan in freezer, stir every hour. When it is slushy, stir in brandy and crystallized ginger. Divide the sherbet into 6 dessert dishes and return to freezer. (The sherbet will not be hard frozen.).
Makes 6 servings.

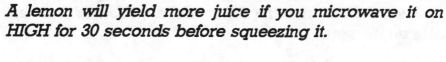

A lemon will yield more juice if you microwave it on HIGH for 30 seconds before squeezing it.

BERRY CUSTARD PARFAIT

2 cups raspberries, fresh or frozen
2 cups blueberries   "
2 cups strawberries   "
1/4 cup sugar
2 8-oz pkgs instant vanilla pudding (or
    double microwave Cream Pie filling)

Hull, wash, (or thaw) and sprinkle berries with sugar. Make pudding according to package directions, or microwave Cream Pie filling. Divide strawberries into 8 parfait glasses. Spoon half of pudding into glasses on top of berries. Divide the blueberries for the 3rd layer; 4th layer, pudding; top layer, raspberries. Serves 8.

Very pretty, and one of those formulas that can be adapted to what you have, either fresh or frozen - peaches, blackberries, mangos, even bananas and apples.

LEMON SAUCE MICROWAVE

1 cup sugar
1 large egg
1 tsp grated lemon peel
1/3 cup fresh lemon juice

1/2 cup butter

Melt butter in 1-quart glass bowl in microwave on HIGH for 30 to 45 seconds. Whisk in sugar, lemon peel and juice, then egg. Blend well. Microwave on MEDIUM-HIGH, 2 to 3 minutes, stirring after each minute, to dissolve sugar and thicken sauce.
The sauce should be served warm, but it may be made ahead and reheated with caution -(microwave on MEDIUM 30 seconds at a time until warm.) Makes 1 2/3 cups.

A favorite over gingerbread. When you use packaged mix for gingerbread, add 1 teaspoon of cinnamon and 1/2 cup chopped pecans to mix before adding liquid.

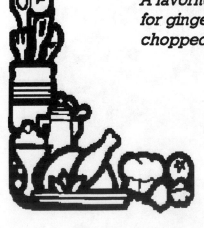

CARAMEL SAUCE MICROWAVE

1 cup brown sugar
1/2 cup whipping cream

1/4 cup butter

Melt butter in a 4-cup glass measuring bowl in the microwave on HIGH for 30 to 60 seconds. Whisk in sugar and cream; microwave on HIGH for 2 to 2 1/2 minutes, stirring after 1 minute. Sauce should be bubbly and beginning to thicken.
Makes 1 1/2 cups.

This is to be served warm, but it may be made ahead and reheated with caution. Try MEDIUM for 30 seconds.

Almost anything is better with caramel sauce - ice cream, gingerbread, bananas, angel food cake, vanilla pudding, etc.

RUM SAUCE MICROWAVE

1/2 cup sugar
1 egg
3 TBS dark rum

6 TBS butter

Melt butter in a 2-cup glass measure in microwave on HIGH for 30 to 60 seconds. Whisk in sugar, then egg. Microwave on MEDIUM 1 1/2 to 2 1/2 minutes, stirring after each minute and scraping down sides of bowl. Sugar should be dissolved and sauce thickened. Strain out any particles of cooked egg. Stir in rum. Serve warm. Makes 1 cup.

Try this to make an ordinary ice cream or cake festive. It is also good on fruit such as bananas or peaches.

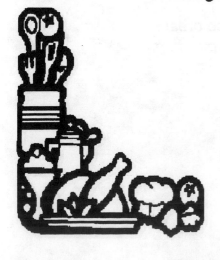

INDEX

He had been eight years upon a project for extracting sun-beams out of cucumbers, which were to be put into vials hermetically sealed, and let out to warm the air in raw inclement summers.

Jonathan Swift, 1726

ORDER FORM

Postal Orders: Cimarron Press, P.O. Box 22007-101, Santa Fe, NM 87502-2007 Phone orders:(505) 473-7771

Please send *Cooking with a Handful of Ingredients*. I understand that I may return any books for a full refund.

Name:_____

Address:_____

City:_____ State:_____ Zip:_____

Price: $15.95 per book
Sales tax:
Please add $0.98 for each book shipped to New Mexico addresses
Shipping:
Book rate: $2.50 for the first book and $1.00 for each additional book(Surface shipping may take three to four weeks)
Air Mail: $4.00 per book
Payment: Check or Money Order

ORDER FORM

Postal Orders: Cimarron Press, P.O. Box 22007-101, Santa Fe, NM 87502-2007 Phone: (505) 473-7771

Please send *Cooking with a Handful of Ingredients*. I understand that I may return any books for a full refund.

Name:_____

Address:_____

City:_____ State:_____ Zip:_____

Price: $15.95 per book
Sales tax:
Please add $0.98 for each book shipped to New Mexico addresses
Shipping:
Book rate: $2.50 for the first book and $1.00 for each additional book(Surface shipping may take three to four weeks)
Air Mail: $4.00 per book
Payment: Check or Money Order